PRAISE FROM HIS
A PH.D.'S REVERIE: ~~THE LETTERS~~

A Ph.D.'s Reverie tells a deeply personal story about Frank Guittard that also pays homage to contemporary changes at Baylor University, broader changes in the United States, and timeless questions about family relationships, personal identity, cultural pressures, and career ambitions. The book includes personal letters, an illustrated poem, an essay, short biographies, and numerous photographs - there is something for everybody to enjoy, and it all comes together wonderfully!

> KENNA LANG ARCHER, Ph.D.: Assistant Professor of History, San Angelo State University; author of *Unruly Waters: A Social and Environmental History of the Brazos River* (New Mexico).

A Ph.D.'s Reverie: The Letters is a creative and unusual piece of nonfiction which appeals on many levels. It represents an artful and compelling interweaving of correspondence between a college history professor and his family while on sabbatical to obtain his Ph.D. with fascinating editor's notes capturing the evolution controversy raging at Baylor University in Waco during the 1920s...

> KEN BAIN, Ph.D.: president of the Best Teachers' Institute and author of *What the Best College Teachers Do* (Harvard) and *What the Best College Students Do* (Harvard), and of the forthcoming *Super Courses* (Princeton); a former professor at Northwestern, Vanderbilt, NYU, and the University of Texas.

In the middle ages, the terror inspired by the final examinations to receive one's degree was compared to the Last Judgment. Guittard, with an equal sense of dread compares his German language proficiency test to a very steep hill, his comprehensive examinations to the Matterhorn, and the completion of the thesis to Mt. Everest. Daunting indeed...

> JEFFREY HAMILTON, Ph.D.: Professor of History and past department chair, Baylor University; Vice-Provost for Global Engagement, and Jo Murphy Chair in International Education; author of *The Plantagenets: History of a Dynasty (Continuum).*

...Charles Guittard has painted a clear and succinct story of the period when Baylor University securely transitioned to growing in national stature during the groundbreaking presidency of Samuel Palmer Brooks, 1902-1931.

> GEORGE GAWRYCH, Ph.D.: Professor of History, Baylor University; author of *The Young Attaturk: From Ottoman Soldier to Statesman of Turkey* (I. B. Tauris).

...I especially recommend these letters for their sincere humanity: the loving exchanges between husband and wife, the heartfelt admiration between father and son, and Frank Guittard's grappling with the challenges and joys of graduate studies.

> TIMOTHY GRUNDMEIER, Ph.D.: Professor of History, Martin Luther College.

The letters of Frank Guittard are wonderful sources for illuminating multiple aspects of American history, especially the history of higher education but also the history of the family, the South and West, economics, medicine, and religion. In this volume, Charles Guittard has included helpful notes that place these letters in their wider American context.

> ANDREA L. TURPIN, Ph.D.: Author of *A New Moral Vision: Gender, Religion, and the Changing Purposes of American Higher Education, 1837-1917* (Cornell)

...The richly edited letters reveal multiple threads of interest: F.G. Guittard's time spent at Stanford University, where he would earn a Ph.D. in history; his wife Josie's successful efforts to maintain the household and care for her family in Waco; glimpses into academic life at Baylor University; and the cultural-religious clash of the divisive 1920s evolution controversy...A Ph.D.'s Reverie provides an endearing and eminently enjoyable portrait of a family separated temporarily by distance, but bound together by common beliefs and bonds.

> KIMBERLY R. KELLISON, Ph.D.: Associate Dean of the College of Arts and Sciences, Associate Professor of History & past department chair, Baylor University.

...A history professor at Baylor in the first half of the twentieth century, [Frank Guittard] was...an "ordinary person teaching at a small quiet private college." But in this illuminating and entertaining collection of letters from Frank Guittard and his family, readers get a sense of the significance of the ordinary. On the one hand, the letters serve as a valuable primary source for understanding aspects of American life in the 1920s. On the other hand, there is a timeless quality present in these letters: the desire for love, the quest for personal and intellectual growth, the concern for health and economic stability. For historians interested in Baylor University, central Texas, or Southern Baptists—or for "ordinary" individuals looking for inspiration from the past—A Ph.D.'s Reverie (second edition) is highly recommended.

> PAUL EMORY PUTZ, Ph.D.: Assistant Director Sports Ministry/Chaplaincy Program, George W. Truett Theological Seminary, Baylor University; forthcoming book to be published by Oxford.

There are no richer sources for meaningful cultural history than family letters. Superbly presented and edited, the deeply personal letters between Frank Guittard and his family reveal honest emotions and opinions on concerns ranging from American society and academia to politics and religious disputes during the "roaring" 1920s. A Ph.D.'s Reverie is a delight to read and ponder.

> T. MICHAEL PARRISH, Ph.D.: The Linden G. Bowers Professor of American History, Baylor University; co-author of *Brothers in Gray: The Civil War Letters of the Pierson Family* (LSU) and author of Richard Taylor: *Soldier Prince of Dixie* (North Carolina).

...this illuminating volume of Guittard family correspondence...offers fascinating glimpses of a surprisingly broad range of issues in early 20th century American history, including the history of family life, academic culture, and religious conflict.

> THOMAS S. KIDD, Ph.D.: Distinguished Professor of History, James Vardaman Endowed Professor of History, Baylor University; author of *Benjamin Franklin: The Religious Life of a Founding Father* (Yale) and with Barry Hankins, *Baptists in America* (Oxford).

In our age of higher education headaches and increasing numbers of non-traditional students, the remarkable story of Frank Guittard from nearly a century ago shows that these trials are nothing new...Frank spent [seven] years late in life to earn a Ph.D. and set an example of academic excellence for others at his embattled school, Baylor University...For all who feel ordinary and overwhelmed as they struggle through higher education, Frank's story is an inspiration...

BRENDAN JONES PAYNE, Ph.D.: Assistant Professor of History, North Greenville University; author of *Christians Defying Jim Crow* forthcoming from LSU.

A Ph.D.'s Reverie: The Letters... is an impressive combination of collegial, social, and religious history. At the heart is the extraordinary story of an ordinary man.... Readers, especially those currently in graduate school, will find much to admire and empathize with as the story of Frank Guittard and his family, told through their own words, unfolds. A Ph.D.'s Reverie is a reminder that no matter the best laid plans, the unexpected has a tendency to happen...

TAYLOR KNIPHFER: Ph.D. student in history, The Catholic University of America.

This volume offers a vivid window onto the ordinary life of a small-town, professor's household in the early twentieth century. It combines historical scholarship with primary source selections and a lively, poetic engagement with family history. This second edition now includes a wealth of letters from 1920 to 1930. These letters are invaluable records of family relationships during the 1920s, showcasing unique details of daily life along with flirtation and gender roles, the trials of academia, and a generous helping of wit and humor...The every-day details preserved, from lawn-mowing to dissertation typing, beautifully document the material conditions of the era. Charles Guittard's meticulous research, insightful notes, and biographical sketches provide an essential road map throughout.

JOSEPH STUBENRAUCH, Ph.D.: Associate Professor of History and Graduate Program Director, Baylor University; author of *The Evangelical Age of Ingenuity in Industrial Britain* (Oxford).

This is the story in family correspondence and verse of one of the seminal figures in the history of the Department of History at Baylor University. And, what a story it is...

BARRY HANKINS, Ph.D.: Professor of History and Department Chair, Baylor University; author of *Woodrow Wilson: Ruling Elder, Spiritual President* (Oxford) and of *God's Rascal: J. Frank Norris and the Beginnings of Southern Fundamentalism* (Kentucky).

...This book is a reminder that some elements of graduate work in history are timeless, such as the inevitable "hours among musty smelling volumes." Along the way, the reader also encounters the quotidian elements of life in rural America at the turn of the twentieth century. But in the midst of all this, Charles Francis Guittard has produced a work that reminds us of the human element of history. The Guittard letters include family, love, grief, humor, and recollection, all a testament to Frank Guittard's reminder that "little things go to make up life."

NICHOLAS PRUITT, Ph.D.: Assistant Professor of History, Eastern Nazarene College, Quincy, Massachusetts.

Readers will find the collection of letters presented in Guittard's expanded edition of A Ph.D.'s Reverie engaging and entertaining. From colorful biographical poetry, penned by Charles Francis Guittard and illustrated by Grace Elizabeth Daniel, to the captivating prose of letters exchanged by Frank and Josie during their years apart. The editor's notes, which are used to contextualize the correspondence and add depth to the reader's knowledge, add great value here to experience a fuller exploration of the period.

STEPHEN M. SLOAN, Ph.D.: Associate Professor of History and Director of the Institute of Oral History, Baylor University; co-editor of *Listening on the Edge...* (Oxford) and co-editor of *Tattooed on My Soul...* (Texas A&M).

PRAISE FROM OTHERS FOR
A PH.D.'S REVERIE: THE LETTERS

Charles Guittard has written a book that is so meticulously detailed you almost feel as if they were a part of your own family. By the end I found myself finding similarities between the characters and my own person... He personalized each character so they were relatable and I cared about them. And if you went to Baylor, it is probably a delight to see history through the eyes and ears of the writers of these letters...

HESHA ABRAMS: Attorney-Mediator, Dallas, Texas.

Through painstaking editing and commentary, as well as familial devotion, Charles Guittard has provided us with an important chronicle of an interesting life in transition. In the process, he also gives us a snapshot of an historical era and the issues that shaped it. As an academic, I was particularly taken with the efforts of President Samuel Palmer Brooks to preserve academic freedom by defending Baylor against the fundamentalists of that era...

JAMES ALFINI: Professor of Law and Dean Emeritus, South Texas College of Law, Houston, Texas; co-author of *Judicial Conduct and Ethics, Fifth Edition* (LexisNexis).

Editor Charles Guittard has done an excellent job of assembling the correspondence of his paternal grandfather Frank Guittard...Many of the letters are between his grandfather and grandmother... The photos show a very serious academic, but the letters reveal a very touching tenderness. And there are several instances that give the flavor of the early 1900s, including one in which Frank compliments his "wifie" for installing an indoor toilet in a rent house they own. Next, he says in a 1928 letter, that an indoor bathtub "will probably be the next requirement."

JON R. BAUMAN: author of *Santa Fe Passage* (Truman Talley) and *The Sovereigns and the Admiral: A Biography of Isabel, Ferdinand and Columbus* (Epigram).

If one wonders about the challenges of life in America in the late nineteenth and early twentieth century, and seeks to understand and empathize with those who achieved a measure of success entirely on their own, through the time-tested means of higher education, hard work, persistence, and love of family, A Ph.D.'s Reverie tells that story of dedication and sacrifice through its assemblage of letters, illustrations, photographs, and a poem.

TALMAGE BOSTON: author of *Cross-Examining History: A Lawyer Gets Answers From the Experts About Our Presidents* and *1939: Baseball's Tipping Point* (both Bright Sky).

In equal parts historical drama, family anecdotes and philosophical musing, the Second Edition is a completely unique form of biography. The story of Frank Guittard, a seemingly ordinary man who became an academic through sheer perseverance, is told from a wide variety of perspectives: through poetry and art, through the subject's own words, through his family's correspondence from the time, and held together by the observations of Frank's grandson, the author, who both searches for answers about...family history, as well as answers to the broader questions of life that affect us all. To what extent can our lives be planned? Or are our plans merely attempts to bring order to the outside forces that inevitably sway our destinies?

CHARLES W. McGARRY: Former Chief Justice of the Dallas Court of Appeals; appellate, entertainment, and real estate law, north Texas.

Charles Guittard opens up a life and an era in these pages. In the linked stories of Frank Guittard's quest to become a great scholar and Baylor University's fight to be a great university, we learn about a man, a family, an institution, and a nation. Historians and history buffs alike will find much to admire here.

GREG GARRETT, Ph.D.: Professor of English, Baylor University, 2013 Baylor Centennial Professor; author of *Free Bird* (Austin Heights) and *The Prodigal* (Zondervan).

This masterful, interwoven portrait of a brilliant teacher of history at Baylor University is a genuine treasure. The poetry, the warm tender drawings, the carefully selected letters and the commentary provide a deep insight into the life, work and times of Frank Guittard (1867-1950). One also gains a deep appreciation for the struggles of Baylor University during the Brooks presidency which covered the first third of the Twentieth Century. A highly recommended read!

WILLIAM F. COOPER, Ph.D.: Professor Emeritus, Philosophy, and former Dean of the College of Arts & Sciences, Baylor University.

Frank Gevrier Guittard was definitely a "man in earnest." He knew how crucial it is to preserve history; he pursued his Ph.D. not only to support his family but to teach future generations of history students the value of using their knowledge of history to question the world around them. His letters to his family in fact recorded for future readers many of the significant events occurring while he labored at Stanford. All the while his friend and colleague, President of Baylor University, Samuel P. Brooks, made his own history defending Baylor's integrity over the question of teaching evolution theory in the 1920s, which had plunged Baptists into the rancorous debate between Christian fundamentalists and the scientific community.

CAROL CHAMBERS GIBSON, M.A.: Kilgore College, English professor and author of *Rossetti's Apologetics* and *Rossetti's Reformation of Religion* in the University of Oxford's Literary Journal.

[A Ph.D.'s Reverie: The Letters]...recounts the life of ...[Frank] Guittard, a long time professor at Baylor University in Waco, Texas, through Guittard family letters. How [Guittard] struggled and earned his PhD... told against the backdrop of academic conflicts at Baylor during the administration of President Samuel Palmer Brooks. This story includes the conflict between Brooks and J. Frank Norris, the teaching of evolution, the bid to relocate the university to Dallas and several other interesting threads...highly recommend this book.

MIKE MAGERS, CPA: Ablon and Company, Dallas, Texas; manager, Texas History Notebook at texoso66.com, a blog about Texas.

A Ph.D.'s Reverie: The Letters is an illustrated work of nonfiction by Charles F. Guittard...The book has many interesting sub-plots concerning other members of Frank's family—including courtships, mountain climbing episodes, health and financial issues, and the intellectual pursuits of the two sons who went into the law as a profession. One of the primary sub-plots focuses on the fact that Baylor's president allowed professors to explain, not advocate, Darwin's theory of evolution. But because this was the 1920s (and in the same era as the notorious "Scopes Monkey Trial" in Tennessee) and because Baylor was a Baptist institution--there being at that time fundamentalists among Baptists who considered the theory of evolution to be anti-Biblical, Baylor's president was regularly vilified by enemies in speeches, radio broadcasts, and sectarian periodicals. Fortunately for Baylor, academic freedom won out.

DAN S. BOYD: trial and appellate lawyer, Dallas, Texas; one of the twenty board members of the Board of Trustees of the Franklin D. Roosevelt Presidential Library in Hyde Park, New York; author of *Grand Aspirations* (Adlibbed Ltd).

Every Baylor graduate should read this story of Frank Guittard, Baylor University history department chair, who undertook to obtain his Ph.D. in his late fifties at the request of his president Samuel P. Brooks, who recruited Frank Guittard and other teachers who appreciated Brooks' vision of Baylor eventually becoming a major university. Those faculty members in turn became his steadfast supporters. Together with Brooks, and in part because of Brooks, Brooks' faculty was motivated to offer "the best that has been thought and said," Matthew Arnold's classic definition of education. Their successors joined by alumni must remain vigilant to guarantee that Baylor continues to strive to offer an education that is untainted by sectarian ideologues and which holds fast to academic freedom.

LINDA BUNNELL, Ph.D.: Chancellor Emerita, University of Colorado, University of Wisconsin.

...With the presentation and explanation of letters from almost 100 years ago, the book provides a vivid picture of a gifted man and his family in a time of turmoil and development for Baylor University. In the author/editor's hands, the old letters bring to life for today's reader how an established professor in Texas courted his second wife after being widowed, sought to guide his growing sons with a fatherly hand, and worked very hard over multiple summers to earn his Ph.D. at Stanford University. I particularly enjoyed the professor's letters describing the research, writing, and advisor meetings that went into his dissertation—all in an era without computers or the internet...

W. JOHN GLANCY: Retired attorney, Dallas, Texas and former briefing clerk to U.S. Supreme Court Justice Byron "Whizzer" White.

I just finished reading A Ph.D.'s Reverie: The Letters...and was surprised to find that it is much more than an historical depiction of a...hard-working professor. It starts with a whirlwind love story followed by the narrative of an exhausting academic marathon, supplemented with a carefully researched account of the religious and social issues that framed men's lives in the 1920s, a description of the daily activities of the family members during this decade including selling eggs by the professor's wife to other faculty members and making preserves and homemade candy, and the disclosure of the family's private discussions regarding keeping their financial house afloat during challenging economic times.

MADELYN D. KAMEN, DrPH: Retired Associate Dean and Professor, The University of Texas Health Science Center at Houston, Texas.

WHY DO WE NEED TO STUDY HISTORY?

"History is a hill or high point from which alone men see the town in which they live or the age in which they are living."

G. K. Chesterton

"What is today a matter of academic speculation, begins tomorrow to move armies and pull down empires."

J. Gresham Machen

"…History paints us a detailed picture of how society, technology, and government worked way back when so that we can better understand how it works now. It also helps us determine how to approach the future, as it allows us to learn from our past mistakes (and triumphs) as a society…"

Arcadia Publishing and The History Press,
"Why It's Important That We Study History,"
arcadiapublishing.com (2019).

"…History is more than just the living record of nations, leaders, and wars…It's packed with tales of how someone stood up for what they believed in, or died for love, or worked hard to make their dreams come true…"

Arcadia Publishing and The History Press,
"Why It's Important That We Study History,"
arcadiapublishing.com (2019).

"…Why study history? The answer is because we virtually must, to gain access to the laboratory of human experience. When we study it reasonably well, and so acquire some usable habits of mind, as well as some basic data about the forces that affect our own lives, we emerge with relevant skills and an enhanced capacity for informed citizenship, critical thinking, and simple awareness…"

Peter N. Stearns
American Historical Association,
historians.org (1998).

The Second Edition of

A Ph.D.'s Reverie:

The Letters

A Whirlwind Courtship,

A Ph.D. Student's Ordeal

Charles Francis Guittard
Author & Editor

Thomas A. DeShong
Co-editor

Francis "Frank" Gevrier Guittard

First Edition Design Publishing
Sarasota, Florida USA

A Ph.D.'s Reverie, The Letters, A Whirlwind Courtship, A Ph.D. Student's Ordeal, 2ed.
Copyright ©2019 Charles Francis Guittard

ISBN 978-1506-908-21-2 PBK
ISBN 978-1506-908-22-9 EBK

LCCN 2019939469

July 2019

Published and Distributed by
First Edition Design Publishing, Inc.
P.O. Box 17646, Sarasota, FL 34276-3217
www.firsteditiondesignpublishing.com

The original, illustrated, biographical poem concerning Francis ("Frank") Gevrier Guittard with historical notes; the featured piece: 256 excerpted and edited family letters with editor's notes, beginning with the courtship of Frank Guittard and Josie Glenn and concluding with the completion of Frank's quest for a Ph.D. at Stanford University; all framed by a new editor's preface and epilogue.

A Proverb

And Kronos now grown old,
Metis and Tyche did battle each other,
Each to impose her will upon him,
The outcome dark and doubtful,
The impact upon mortals untold.

Kronos - primeval god of time
Metis - goddess of planning, prudence,
    and wise counsel
Tyche - goddess of chance, luck,
    and fortune

Table of Contents

Preface to the Second Edition i

Note to the Reader, The Special Role of the Editor's Notes xiii

Acknowledgments xvii

A Singular Salute xix

Lists of Illustrations, Photographs, and Exemplars.................................... xxi

A Ph.D.'s Reverie 1

Historical Notes on the Poem 17

College Essay, Baylor University, 1894 22

Portraits, Photographs, and Snapshots, The Guittard Family 26

Handwriting Exemplars for the Guittard Correspondence 37

The Letters 49

Photographs: Baylor University and Leland Stanford Junior Universities.............. 321

Discussion Questions and Trivia 332

Epilogue 334

The Guittard Family 335

Baylor Figures in this Volume 336

Tuberculosis, Spinal Meningitis, and Spanish Influenza.................... 338

The State of Tennessee v. John Thomas Scopes and its Aftermath...................... 340

The Evolution Controversy in Texas... 343

The Evolution Controversy in Tennessee and Elsewhere 343

Roosevelt, Conservation, and Environmentalism................................ 344

A Final Note on *A Ph.D.'s Reverie: The Letters* 345

The "Proverb" 346

Appendices 347

Historical Timeline for the Principal Characters................................. 348

Answers to Discussion Questions and Trivia... 351

The Author-Illustrator Collaboration.. 355

A Preview of *The Life & Times of Frank Guittard* 357

Sources 360
Biographies 363
    Charles Francis Guittard, Author and Editor................................. 364
    Grace Elizabeth Daniel, Illustrator 365
    Thomas A. DeShong, Co-Editor.. 366

Author's Postscript to the 2nd Edition of A Ph.D.'s Reverie.................... 367

Index... 368

Dedication

This work is dedicated to the Department of History at Baylor University, the recipients of the Guittard History Fellowship, the recipients of the Guittard-Verlander-Voegtle Scholarship, and all students of history at the college or graduate level, wherever they may be enrolled, particularly those working their way through.

This work is also dedicated to my wife and partner, Patricia Verlander Guittard, who supported the project enthusiastically from beginning to end, even when she was not feeling well, and, finally, to all descendants of Francis ("Frank") Gevrier Guittard and Mamie Welhausen Guittard, but especially including great-great grandchildren Miles, Charlie, Finn, and Katherine, who hopefully one day will be interested in the letters included within and the study of history.

PREFACE TO THE SECOND EDITION

Is adventure just bad planning? Norwegian adventurer and explorer Roald Amundsen thought so, and Frank Guittard would have agreed. Though Frank never traveled outside North America and was a college professor in a small town, he was another kind of adventurer. His original quest, migrating from Ohio to Texas and working his way through college, was accomplished after an exasperatingly long fifteen years. Twenty-five years later, he was engaged in another long-drawn-out mission (1923-1931), this time to secure a Ph.D. from Stanford University. As the fifty-nine-year-old student sat in a Palo Alto apartment during the summer of 1926, his mind frequently turned to his concerns back in Texas, including helping his oldest son plan his career and learn from his father's mistakes. The stakes were high, and Frank wanted every word of advice to count. Frank's thoughts on planning for a career and not being a victim of circumstance, generally encouraging but sometimes regretfully confessing youthful imprudence, are among the sage asides readers will encounter in the Second Edition of *A Ph.D.'s Reverie*.

First, a few words should be said about two of the different hats worn in connection with producing this work. One is the author's hat which arises in connection with the poem "A Ph.D.'s Reverie," the historical notes contained in the First Edition, and with the work-in-progress tentatively titled *The Life & Times of Frank Guittard*, sometimes referred to herein as the *"Life & Times."* The other is the editor's hat which arises in connection with the editor's notes to the excerpted correspondence in the Second Edition. Combining the two editions in this volume has occasionally resulted in references in one or more parts of this work, particularly in this preface and in the acknowledgments section, both to "author" and to "editor." However, it should be made clear that both references are to the same person.

Second, a few more words about what comprises the Second Edition may be in order. *A Ph.D.'s Reverie*, referred to in this work as the First Edition, and *A Ph.D.'s Reverie: The Letters*, referred to as the Second Edition, may be distinguished as follows: the First Edition was an illustrated poem, in places imaginative (i.e., the dream about his mother), but mostly supported by historical fact; the Second Edition, while reprising the poem and the supporting historical facts, primarily features the actual correspondence exchanged between 1920 and 1930 among members of the Guittard family—Francis ("Frank") Gevrier Guittard, Josie (sometimes "Mama Josie") Glenn Guittard, Francis Gevrier Guittard, Jr., and Clarence (sometimes "Sonny Boy") Alwin Guittard. The letters are supplemented with notes from the editor providing context and clarification when appropriate. (See hereinafter the chapter entitled "The Special Role of the Editor's Notes" which discusses the various purposes the notes have in this work which may differ from the customary footnotes appended to letters in a book of correspondence.) It should also be noted that because Frank's letters spend little or no time on the substance of his dissertation, "Roosevelt and Conservation," comment on that subject will be reserved for the Epilogue to this work and *The Life & Times*.

Before addressing the letters, it is fitting to present short, bare-bones biographies for Frank, Josie, Francis, and Clarence, brief descriptions of their personal characteristics to come later in this preface:

> Frank Guittard was an Ohioan born in 1867, the fourth of seven surviving children of a physician-farmer and his Pennsylvania Dutch wife. In 1886, during hard economic times, his parents pushed him out of the nest to seek his fortune in Texas. In 1890, after a string of teaching positions in country schools, he entered Baylor University in Waco, but dropped out after two years when his money ran out. He thereafter worked his way through the University of Chicago primarily by teaching in Texas schools, earning a master's degree in history in 1902. He accepted the first college teaching offer he received after

graduation from Baylor acquaintance Samuel Palmer Brooks, the new president of Baylor. Frank married twice, first to Mamie Welhausen, the mother of his three children: Francis, Charles (who died before his second birthday), and Clarence. After Mamie succumbed to tuberculosis in 1917, Frank married Josie Glenn in 1920. Josie kept the home fires burning while he pursued a Ph.D. from Stanford University between 1923 and 1931 at the bidding of President Brooks. Brooks had a grand vision for Baylor as a major university--which vision required at a minimum that all department chairs have their doctorates.

Josie Glenn, born in 1885, was a Texan from Bronte, the oldest of nine children of a hardscrabble farming couple. She was a teacher, working at schools in Houston, until she married Frank in 1920. Josie was the only mother Clarence ever knew. Josie quickly became a well-liked faculty wife because of her pleasant personality and sense of humor, her willingness to take on responsibility in various organizations, and her opening their home on many occasions to friends and faculty. She strongly supported Frank's pursuit of a Ph.D., managed the household in his absences, and occasionally found books he needed for his dissertation.

Francis Guittard was Frank's oldest son. Born in Waco in 1907, he was a high school student when Frank started his work at Stanford and a young lawyer in Victoria, Texas when Frank received his Ph.D. in 1931.

Clarence Guittard was Frank's youngest son, born in Waco in 1917, two months before his mother Mamie died from tuberculosis. He was probably not yet in school when Frank enrolled at Stanford in 1923 and likely in his last year of junior high school when Frank received his degree.

The letters, which are divided into two groups, are referred to hereafter as "The Courtship Letters" and "The Palo Alto Letters." The Courtship Letters, preceding the periods in Palo Alto, describe the early details of Frank and Josie's romantic encounter, which would likely still have been on his mind while at Stanford. They had been married only three years prior to his first summer at Stanford. The Palo Alto Letters reveal that Frank's thoughts and feelings, or reveries, whether working at the Stanford library or in his room, eating breakfast at The Snow White Creamery or supper at the Mandarin Restaurant, or reflecting on the occasion of receiving his Ph.D., would have gone far beyond an imagined dream encounter with his late mother, a poetic device used at the climax of the poem. The Palo Alto Letters, on the other hand, expose the real life issues Frank, Josie, Francis, and Clarence were facing. Notably, the letters show that while carrying the heavy burden of succeeding in his Ph.D. work, Frank was also bearing concerns about each of his family members, and to some extent about himself—concerns about health, education, career, marriage, household finances, politics, Baylor University, and other matters. Frank felt a keen responsibility to steer Josie, Francis, and Clarence in the right directions, even from his room in Palo Alto.

As to the need for a preface to the Second Edition, the First Edition contained no preface, having been comprised of only a poem of 120 lines, fifteen original hand-drawn illustrations, a few pages of historical notes, a handful of photographs, and only thirty-six pages altogether. Any preface to the First Edition might have been considered vain, odd, or a combination of both. However, with this Second Edition, the need for a preface is now compelling. This new edition of *A Ph.D.'s Reverie* is offered first and foremost to add, through family correspondence, the actual voices, words, and personalities of Frank Guittard, his wife Josie, and his sons Francis Jr. and Clarence, to the original free-verse narrative poem and accompanying historical notes. In fact, the addition of the letters *ipso facto* provides substantial additional context for the "Reverie," including both the recent courtship, indeed the romantic pursuit by Frank of his then wife-to-be Josie, and the details of Frank's academic pursuit of a Ph.D. in Palo Alto beginning in 1923. Accordingly, the additional materials merit comment in a preface.

Second, the preface serves not only to comment on the added content and context provided by the letters, but to tie together all the pieces of the Second Edition, namely, the poem, the illustrations, the letters, the editor's notes, Frank's college essay, and the epilogue, along with a number of additional photographs, to the central theme they all illuminate. The theme of *A Ph.D.'s Reverie,* both in the First and Second Editions, is the stressful time period from 1923 through 1930 in which Frank, newly re-married after a whirlwind courtship, labored away in relative isolation in Palo Alto to earn his Ph.D. from Stanford. Frank's reveries in that period would inevitably have drawn upon a number of his memories, including growing up on the family farm in Ohio, traveling to Texas as a land scout, courting and marrying his first wife Mamie Welhausen, losing three family members prematurely (his mother, his second son, and his wife), courting his second wife Josie Glenn, and pursuing a Ph.D. from Stanford as a student in residence away from his new wife and two sons for twenty-three months.

Additionally, because Frank Guittard was nothing if not deeply reflective and inclined toward reverie his entire life, not simply during the time spent in Palo Alto, the editor has also included an untitled essay Frank composed as a Baylor student in 1894. For the sake of convenience, the editor has titled the essay, "The Caravan Across the Land of Toil." This work is the closest thing to a statement of Frank's personal philosophy of life in 1894. Frank likely never strayed far from the aphorism expressed in this essay that a *"system conquers all things"* and *"a reward awaits all who are loyal to duty."* This "system and duty" mantra appears to have influenced all his major decisions after leaving Baylor. Over thirty years later and over the course of six summers in Palo Alto, Frank had a lot of time to ruminate on the path he had taken in his life's journey across "The Land of Toil," consciously or otherwise, intentionally or as the result of circumstance or necessity, and how well that path had served him and his family.

But why initially compose a biographical poem (the First Edition) and why is Frank Guittard's life a worthy subject for a poem or for study and the family correspondence worthy of publication? As to why a poem, the long answer is that *The Life & Times* book project of the author about

Frank Guittard, for which the author had commenced research in 1978, had gradually become so time-intensive that it sometimes seemed that one lifetime might not be enough to bring the work to completion. Accordingly, it seemed desirable in the short term to produce at least a fragment of Frank's story that could be realized more rapidly, the poem being the chosen form to set a piece of the narrative. The choice of a narrative poem, rather than a brief prose summary of Frank's life & times, was based on the fact that Frank's story could not be easily reduced to a brief summary. On the other hand, a poem could be of almost any length without succumbing to the temptation to tell the whole story, with poetic license permitting the author to approach the narrative from a myriad of angles.

As to why a life & times of Frank Guittard and his correspondence with his family might be interesting, Frank's life as a subject for a much larger work had actually started percolating in the mind of the author when he first happened to read a batch of the Palo Alto Letters. At that time, it seemed that an interesting life & times could possibly be researched and written, not because Frank was a genius, a brilliant military leader, a prominent elected representative of the people, an award-winning scientist, or even a nationally known historian and author, for he was none of those things, and was in fact, in most ways, an ordinary person teaching at a small quiet private college. There are several possible reasons that Frank's life might be interesting. The first is that while in most respects Frank was for the largest part of his life an ordinary college professor living a simple life in a relatively quiet college town, a sort of a turn-of-the-century central Texas "Mr. Chips,"* is that both groups of letters reveal a lot about what Frank was like as a person and what was going on in his life and that of his family one hundred years ago. To open a book of family letters can be to travel back in time and almost eavesdrop on a family living in a different era, provided the letters are interesting and excerpted with care.

Second, the letters themselves are appealing because, with the help of both the letters and the photographs, the reader is personally introduced to the four principal players in Frank's story through their own words and physical likenesses. The character portraits which ultimately have emerged of the four Guittards from all available sources available to the editor, but not limited to the letters, are as follows:

Frank: The methodical, disciplined, cautious, and tenacious scholar, dismissive of blatherskites and flannelmouths, who generally did not verbalize his feelings, but could be outwardly emotional on occasion, sensitive to affronts to his dignity or to his sense of justice. Though in his letters to family he could be eloquent and often passionate, he tended to be a bit stiff in person with a preference for solitude and reading rather than social interaction. When he had to make important decisions, he was inclined to turn inward rather than solicit advice. He was not afraid of hard manual labor including farm work and painting houses. He loved animals, particularly dogs and cats, and the outdoors. Imaginative and an aficionado of art, opera, and classical compositions for piano, he had a broad interest in other cultures and countries including those in the Far East. He was a life-long Democrat who sympathized with working people, particularly those who had to work their way through school. Perhaps as much as anything, he had a voracious appetite for reading about the facts of the past which combined happily with an unpredictable, dry wit. Frank was fifty-six through sixty-four years of age during the period of the Palo Alto years (1923-1931).

Josie: The spontaneous, funny, energetic, optimistic, devoted, maternal, and loyal team-player, with an affectionate, playful, and personable nature. She was a natural ice-breaker. Careful with money and a saver, she was able to run a busy household with ease. She was more provincial than Frank although she ultimately traveled to Europe after Frank's death; he never did. Josie enjoyed attending musical concerts and educational lectures. Josie was thirty-eight through forty-five years of age during the Palo Alto years.

Francis: The bright, cocky, unusually competitive, high-achieving, athletic first son, with strong verbal and advocacy skills. He was ambitious and risk-taking, and welcomed mental and physical challenges where he could test and compare himself with others. He had a strong need for approval from Frank. To some extent, he mirrored characteristics of Frank. For a number of years, he studied piano and played compositions by classical composers. Francis was fifteen through twenty-three years of age during the Palo Alto years.

Clarence: The reflective youngest son with a passion for reading and strong writing skills. He was also bright and a high-achiever. Clarence was collaborative, affectionate, somewhat reticent, careful not to hurt others' feelings by a careless word, and a lover of animals. He also mirrored some of Frank's characteristics. He played French horn in the Waco High School and Baylor University bands. He was six through fourteen years of age during the Palo Alto years.

There is a third reason why the story and family correspondence of an ordinary person like Frank Guittard may be intriguing: Frank's story itself (to be expounded upon and fleshed out further in *The Life & Times*) is positively out of the ordinary. Frank, after finishing his early schooling and after concentrating his aptitudes on improvements to the family farm for a year or so, was gently but abruptly pushed out of the Ohio family nest due to his family's financial and economic circumstances. The result was that he was effectively transplanted from his Ohio home to Texas at nineteen years of age over 130 years ago, his ostensible mission to scout available land and suitable environs for a possible family move. Unfortunately, neither his mother nor his father would ever see Texas, and Frank would be surprised by the news of his mother's illness and sudden untimely death, never having seen her again after moving to Texas.

Thereafter, Frank struggled with little or no financial help for fifteen years to obtain a college education. With limited guidance as to possible career paths, his original desire to follow his father into medicine was denied for lack of funds, thus propelling his decision to become a teacher. Oddly enough, he received his first offer of employment as a college teacher only after a curious incident in a college chapel service at Baylor in which a small dog was pitched out a third-story window by the college president. The chapel incident precipitated a student protest and the president's prompt resignation, thereafter giving rise to the election of President Samuel Palmer Brooks, an acquaintance of Frank's from their Baylor days. Brooks, within a matter of days and before returning to Waco to take up his new position, made a job offer to Frank. The next major life changes for Frank came fifteen years later, when, within a matter of months, he lost both a son and a wife to contagion and ever afterwards was anxious about the danger of infectious disease striking his family.

Finally, Frank, now in his late fifties through his early sixties, in order to pursue a doctorate, for six summers, a winter and a spring, lived apart from his family. His family at the time included a new wife and a young son he had already been separated from for the first four years of his life. Moreover, at Stanford Frank was thirty years older than most of his fellow graduate students and was likely the old man in most of his classes. From Palo Alto, Frank also leveraged his greater life experience to attempt to steer his oldest son's career choice and preparation for that career. His work completed, he returned to Baylor with his doctorate to teach into his eighties as Baylor's oldest active faculty member and continued his decades-long service as grand marshal of Baylor's Annual Commencement Exercises.

The final, and perhaps the most important, reason the letters are appealing is their universal character. The matters they discuss, i.e., engaging in a whirlwind "won't take no for an answer" courtship, learning to drive a car, treating the family's health problems, going to the movies, paying department store bills, taking voice lessons vs. taking piano lessons, preferring some breeds of chickens to others, dealing with tenants who are slow in paying their rent, hiring domestic help for the household, mowing the lawn, paying the church pledge, sleeping in an upper berth on the train, and more, all have an "everyman" feel to them. Moreover, the letters reveal a parent's (Frank's) concern that son Francis make the correct choices regarding a career and how to prepare for that career, a subject that Frank felt keenly about. One of Frank's pet subjects, based on his own experience and intense reflection, was the importance of using time wisely when pursuing a life goal. Frank's letters to his younger son Clarence, on the other hand, reveal his desire to connect with a son fifty years younger than he was, particularly by sharing or making up stories about dogs, cats, and other animals, and encouraging Clarence's penmanship, writing skills, and swimming prowess.

Moreover, the family's everyday correspondence covers a wide range of issues interesting to modern day readers, some letters likely to elicit laughter while others will provoke sighs or sympathy or even groans, but always a feeling of recognition, as in "I've been there too." The letters include accounts of Josie banging her head on a cousin's auto dome light, requiring stitches and an overnight hospital stay; making copious batches of plum preserves, plum butter, and jelly for the fruit closet; repeatedly treating Clarence's obstinate outbreak of poison oak contracted at camp; reporting faithfully on the egg production of the resident chickens (in the backyard chicken coop) intended to make a few extra dollars for the household; relaying Francis' efforts at managing his adolescent skin condition with Fleischmann's Yeast, and all the other topics of their lives during those twenty-three months.

In addition to whatever interest the reader may have in Frank Guittard or the family letters, the compelling historical context of the letters may also be of note. Both the Courtship Letters and the Palo Alto Letters are set during the period in which the controversy over teaching evolution theory was roiling the faithful back in Texas, and generally throughout the Protestant denomination, but especially among Southern Baptists. The letters, in combination with the editor's notes to the Palo Alto Letters, indicate that there were, at least for our consideration, two or more serious struggles in the 1920s proceeding simultaneously and ostensibly independently: first, Frank's determined campaign and lonely ordeal to earn his Ph.D. at Stanford University, and second, Baylor University President Brooks' struggle to protect Baylor and its faculty against the charges of heresy brought by a charismatic archenemy. Much more about these two struggles will be revealed in the letters and about the extent, if any, to which each struggle may have impacted the other, or, as will become clearer in the editor's notes, were both streams flowing concurrently from the same river. (Also see "The Special Role of the Editor's Notes" infra regarding a fuller explanation for the use of editor's notes in developing parallel time tracks for Frank's struggles at Stanford, on the one hand, and President Brooks' struggles back in Waco on the other.) It should be stated again that by taking on the role of editor, the author is now wearing two hats and that most of his efforts in the production of this particular volume will be that of editor since it is comprised chiefly of original correspondence.)

A Ph.D.'s Reverie: The Letters also contains other features not included in the First Edition, such as a group of discussion questions; an historical timeline for the principal characters; a short history of the author-illustrator collaboration with respect to the poem; an epilogue wrapping up the histories of the principal characters in the poem and the letters, the history of the development of a cure for tuberculosis, and the resolution of the controversy over the teaching of evolution; and a preview of *The Life & Times* work-in-progress.

Another question that one might have about this volume is whether it constitutes a hagiographic exercise. Putting aside the fact that the primary feature of the Second Edition is comprised of two groups of excerpted letters, the editor will just say that his intent is to present Frank Guittard's story and the family letters as objectively as possible.

It is hoped that this Second Edition will interest history students, as well as those readers who have never thought of themselves as history students, and pique their curiosity about this central Texas Mr. Chips. It is intended to resonate especially with graduate students, whatever their fields of study, pursuing their degrees years after completing their undergraduate educations, many of them like Frank Guittard--at universities far from home, missing their loved ones, and occasionally lost in their own reveries, perhaps about publishing their theses or dissertations, or possibly about a long-needed break to that scenic hideaway they have been promising their partners.

In particular, careful readers of the letters, will be able to discover the answers to each of the following questions:

What economic forces were at work in 1886 that resulted in Frank leaving Ohio for Texas?

What courtship strategy did Frank Guittard employ where his wife Josie was concerned?

What vocation do the letters suggest Frank thought at one point he probably should have pursued instead of teaching?

What impact did disease have on Frank's life and on the lives of his family members?

What impact did the evolution controversy at Baylor have on Frank's life, career, and his pursuit of a Ph.D. at Stanford?

How was Frank able to cope with his feelings of loneliness arising from his separation from his family while working on his Ph.D.?

What does the reader learn about Frank's competitive side from the letters?

Was Frank's decision not to attempt publication of his dissertation, in hindsight, a mistake?

Finally, *what does the reader learn about Frank as a planner?*

Charles Francis Guittard

[*Editor's note: Arthur Chipping ("Mr. Chips") is the central character in the 1933 novella Goodbye, Mr. Chips by James Hilton about a popular teacher in an English boarding school for boys. In the novella, Chips is initially an earnest but unremarkable teacher who fortuitously meets and then marries a vibrant young woman who brings him out of his shell. Unfortunately, their marriage is brief and ends tragically when she and their child die in childbirth. Although the lives and personalities of Mr. Chips and Frank Guittard are strikingly similar in some ways, in others they are decidedly different as will become evident from the letters presented in this work.*]

NOTE TO THE READER, THE SPECIAL ROLE OF THE EDITOR'S NOTES

In this volume the editor's notes are atypical. Among the reasons are those below.

We believe both the letters and the editor's notes tell important stories.

It is important to note that the stories and over-arching narrative told in *A Ph.D.'s Reverie: The Letters*, do not simply unfold in the family letters themselves, but in the editor's notes as well. This is by design and by necessity. In a real sense, the editor's notes in this work are not the usual numbered, often mind-numbing, dense litany of citations to sources, accompanied by brief, sometimes lengthy, supplemental comments and asides. Instead, these editor's notes are organic and essential pieces of the work as a whole. The editor's view is that the typical footnotes tend to be overlooked by most readers and are simply skipped over in order to return the reader to the big picture narrative presented in more appealing paragraphs in much larger print. The editor's own experience with the average editor's notes is that they are there mostly for the edification of the scholarly reader, but where the ordinary reader is concerned, they may act as a road sign warning the reader to detour back to the main highway to avoid the slow-going, muddy patch toward the bottom of a page.

The editor's notes, however, do not purport to tell everything.

In the introductory paragraphs before the letters below, we mention that the editor does not intend to set forth in editor's notes everything about certain disputes, controversies, or matters addressed in the letters and the notes, but just enough to provide the background for the stories in the letters, including what was happening behind-the-scenes but not mentioned in the letters. More than that would be beyond the scope of this work.

The editor's notes also serve as a fifth voice.

The editor's notes in this work in fact represent a kind of fifth voice, an unseen fellow traveler, or, perhaps even at times, a guide of sorts for the reader, through the lives of the Guittard family members in the 1920s. The editor in this case is someone removed by almost a century from nearly all of the events and happenings described in the letters, occasionally weighing in, hopefully in an unobtrusive manner, on thoughts, feelings, or in some cases, memories as to the topics addressed by Frank, Josie, Francis, or Clarence. The editor's notes often speak, with the assistance of deeper research, as well as hindsight, to important events transpiring behind-the-scenes and inevitably impacting their lives, whether the Guittards were fully aware of them or not, which are barely mentioned or perhaps omitted entirely in the letters which have survived.

The usual citations are not needed.

The editor's notes in this work contain no numbered or footnoted paragraphs, few if any citations to authority, no page number references or words in italics, and no asides in tiny print to bog the reader down in what may seem to some readers as scholarly minutiae.

The factual matters stated in the editor's notes are not in question.

The usual citation and comment style of editor's notes has been avoided, not only to improve their accessibility for the reader, but also because, insofar as the editor is aware, the factual content contained in the notes is generally not in dispute and has been settled for many years. There is no cutting-edge scholarly thesis for which the editor is advocating or investigating and no speculative conclusion from undisputed fact. The mission is simply to tell more of the whole story of the lives of Frank Guittard's family members in the 1920s and, insofar as is practical, not to ignore important bits of historical context completely missing or barely mentioned in the letters. If the reader seeks to attain a better understanding for the kinds of authoritative sources the editor consulted for the editorial notes, he or she may always detour to the page entitled "Sources" contained near the end of this work; and then the reader may return to the letters & notes highway.

Finally, why are the incidents in President Samuel Palmer Brooks' struggle in the evolution controversy (and other struggles) set out in editor's notes "on President Brooks' battles" following specific letters when the letters themselves do not always address these matters?

The answer is that Frank Guittard's struggle to obtain his Ph.D. from Stanford and President Brooks' struggle to protect and defend Baylor University from attacks from within and without, proceeded from a common vision, namely, to grow Baylor University from a small, fledgling university into a first-class university with a reputable faculty competitive with universities across the United States. In a sense, Brooks, a graduate of both Baylor and Yale College, was following in the footsteps of former Baylor University president Oscar Henry Cooper, also a graduate of Yale. Frank Guittard was one of a relatively small number of early Baylor faculty who earned master's degrees from the University of Chicago, a world-class university the day it opened in 1892. The University of Chicago, founded largely with the money of Baptist layman John D. Rockefeller, served for a time as the model for Baptists of what a university could be if founded with Baptist financial support and a strong connection with Baptists.

Frank, having earned two degrees from the University of Chicago, shared, along with other faculty at Baylor, President Brooks' vision that Baylor one day would become a premier university. At the University of Chicago, Frank became familiar with what it took to establish a respected university and later, at Stanford University, became familiar with what had made Stanford a major university in its own right. One or more of his letters show he paid close attention to features of college life at Stanford, with the idea of possible improvements that might be implemented back at Baylor, commencement parades in particular. Commencement and homecoming parades were among Frank's special interests. Home-coming for Baylor alumni was in fact an important part of Brooks' vision to build a top-tier university at Baylor and became an annual feature of the Baylor calendar for students and alumni.

Returning to our question, Frank's struggle at Stanford to earn his doctorate simultaneously with President Brooks' struggle back in Waco to defend and grow Baylor, both springing from a common vision for Baylor's growth and development as a university, strongly suggested linking these themes for the reader in some kind of chronological order; parallel time tracks were chosen for this purpose. The stories of both struggles had elements of the dramatic. Both of these struggles were uncertain of outcome, one arising from academic and other challenges, the other from militant opposition from certain individuals and forces.

There can be no doubt, since Frank and President Brooks both shared, though from different vantage points, the same dream for Baylor, each would have been keenly interested in the other's battles, setbacks, and eventual victories as they occurred in real time. Because of that common vision, one can imagine a series of conversations between them in which each discussed what had happened in his world since they last had talked.

Thus, in a sense, Frank's letters back home describing his struggles at Stanford and how Stanford conducted its affairs, on the one hand, and the accounts of President Brooks' struggles, on the other hand, contending with forces back in Waco and elsewhere, are in fact two facets of the same story. The compelling aspects of these different but related stories hopefully are more interesting to the reader by setting the stories out chronologically in the manner chosen by the editor.

ACKNOWLEDGMENTS

This volume is comprised of the original pieces of the First Edition: a biographical poem, pertinent historical notes, and a group of fifteen illustrations. To those pieces the author as editor has added, for this Second Edition, a significant number of family letters which are supplemented by extensive editor's notes, a preface, an epilogue, and other items. This correspondence and the accompanying notes comprise the primary features of what is being called the Second Edition. Because of the large number of pieces in this volume and because of the collaboration involved in the preparation of the pieces comprising the final manuscript, there are many people to acknowledge. Some of the acknowledgments below will be made as author and others as editor, depending on which hat is applicable.

The author would like to express appreciation to Baylor University History faculty Stephen Sloan and Michael Parrish for their feedback on the poem's dramatic structure and Michael Parrish for his suggestions on the visual presentation of the letters and editor's notes; past History Chair Jeffrey Hamilton for his review of the poem which resulted indirectly in the author adding a somewhat "Biercian" opening to the poem (see Ambrose Bierce's "An Occurrence at Owl Creek Bridge"); History Chair Barry Hankins for his review of the editor's notes in this work pertaining to the evolution controversy at Baylor and elsewhere in the 1920s and his review of the epilogue; Associate Dean Kimberly Kellison for her support of the unconventional idea of composing a poem about the History Department's first chair and her editorial suggestions for the preface and the editor's notes in this volume; Baylor University English Department Senior Lecturer Elizabeth Dell for her helpful analysis of the poetic characteristics of the poem and suggestions for improvement; and the poem's talented illustrator, Grace Elizabeth Daniel, a senior in Baylor's Art Department, for fifteen illustrations that brought the poem to life. Those illustrations completed the triad of "collaboration" by three Baylor academic departments with the author/editor in the preparation of the two editions.

The editor would also like to extend a special thanks to numerous staff members of The Texas Collection at Baylor University and to Thomas A. DeShong in particular, Processing Archivist at the W. R. Poage Legislative Library. The editor is indebted to Tommy for his research, constructive criticism, and general support; for his service as co-editor of all the pieces which make up this volume; and for his careful proof-reading of the entire manuscript several times, but particularly the preface, the editor's notes to the letters, and the epilogue. The editor also appreciates the help of Paul Fisher and Geoff Hunt of The Texas Collection in providing certain photographs included in this work.

Additionally, the author would like to acknowledge the enthusiastic support of Senior Director of Development David Cortes for all the Baylor-related writing projects of the author.

The editor would like to note the general assistance of Deborah E. Gordon with First Edition Design Publishing and the final, painstaking pre-publication edit by Kirsten Dolata.

The author would also like to express gratitude to all of the friends and family members who followed the author's blog on Facebook, and thereby provided enormous encouragement to complete the book. The author would also like to acknowledge all Baylor Department of History faculty members and all Guittard History Fellows and Scholars who have taken an interest in this work.

Finally, it should also be acknowledged that without Frank Guittard's foresight, or, more likely, force of habit, in keeping so many records chronicling the phases of his life, but particularly those concerning the periods in residency at Stanford, this work would never have been possible. He could not have known, of course, that his life would be the subject of one or more volumes, and probably would have snorted dismissively at the idea. However, he was, after all, a person who appreciated history and knew that, without documentation, there can be no history.

A Singular Salute

Frank Guittard's four grandsons, from left to right, Philip Guittard, John Guittard, Charles Guittard, and Stephen Guittard, c. 1948 in backyard at 1401 South 8th Street in Waco.

At the heart of this volume lies the family correspondence. The production and processing of the letters is the story of a forty-year collaboration of the four grandsons of Francis ("Frank") Gevrier Guittard and Mamie Welhausen Guittard: Stephen ("Steve") Wood Guittard, the late Philip ("Phil") Alwin Guittard, John Roscoe Guittard, and the editor, Charles Francis Guittard. The family photograph above, dated 1948, shows the four grandsons as young boys. Steve (the oldest, age 12 years) is on the right in a plaid sport coat, Phil (age 9 years) at the left assuming a "Napoleon" pose, John (the youngest, age 3 years) in a dark coat in the center on the first row, and Charles (age 6 years), coatless behind John's left shoulder and squinting into the sun. Steve and Phil are brothers and first cousins of Charles and John, who are brothers.

In 1978, Steve who was living in Michigan at the time, initially called the editor's attention to the existence of a collection of family letters in a storage room in Victoria, Texas, and encouraged him to contact Phil who lived nearby. Phil thereafter opened up that storage room for the editor who drove in from Dallas, arriving after lunch on a bitingly cold, sleety winter day. As the weather continued to grow more icy and forbidding, the editor, in an hour or less with

Phil's help, found the box of letters relating to Frank Guittard and his family, and hurriedly left on the long drive back to Dallas, hoping to beat the worst of the storm out of town. On the way, however, after a couple of hours had passed, the Pontiac blew out a tire when it ran over something sharp on the highway. Fortunately, the editor, who needed a tow, was able to hitchhike a ride into town with four tender-hearted women in a pickup truck, who welcomed him to climb aboard and ride in the truck's chilly open cargo area into the next town.

Back in Dallas the next day, the letters were added to the correspondence the editor had already gathered. John assisted with preserving the letters which were assembled chronologically in notebooks inside protective plastic sleeves. Steve and Phil also helped with fact-checking background particulars for the text of this volume and John with collecting, assembling, identifying, memorializing, and dating family photographs to accompany the letters. Mary Louise Voegtle Guittard, the only granddaughter of Frank Guittard and sister to Charles and John, although not born until 1950 and thus not in the photograph, has been a valuable behind-the-scenes supporter of this "letters" volume and of the legacy of Frank and Josie Guittard.

This singular salute, accordingly, is for Steve, Phil, John, and Mary, whose help and encouragement spurred both the conception and the completion of this volume. The editor hopes his efforts in assembling the second edition of "A Ph.D.'s Reverie" will merit approval even after the passage of a forty-years.

LISTS OF ILLUSTRATIONS, PHOTOGRAPHS, AND EXEMPLARS

List of Illustrations for the Poem

The reporter asks Frank Guittard, the new Ph.D., a question.   2

Frank's mother tends her Ohio garden.   3

Frank and his parents formulate a plan.   4

Frank's physician father receives payment in baskets of corn.   5

Frank and his mother embrace and say their good-byes.   6

Frank and his father ride to the station.   7

Frank and his father shake hands goodbye.   8

Frank boards the Pennsylvania Railroad for Texas.   9

Frank is lost in thought as he gazes out the window.   10

Frank ponders how to reach his paramount goal of a college degree.   11

Two years later: A telegram arrives with sad news about his mother.   12

Forty years later: Frank nods off shortly before 10 p.m.   13

The "Mother" apparition approaches and Frank speaks to it.   14

The Tower Clock strikes 10 p.m., interrupting Frank's dream.   15

The Southern Pacific takes Frank home to Waco.   16

List of Photographs

Photographic portraits and snapshots relating to the Guittards from the family photograph collection:

Dr. Francis Joseph Guittard (c. 1880); age fifty-two years; studio portrait.   17

Lydia Myers Guittard (c. 1880); age fifty years; studio portrait.   17

Guittard Ohio homestead (c. summer 1898): Frank Guittard sitting at far right looking back at Dr. Francis Joseph Guittard standing at far left.   18

Francis ("Frank") Gevrier Guittard (c. 1894); age twenty-seven years; final term as Baylor University student; studio portrait.   19

Pocket watch Frank Guittard won in 1894 as top book salesman; age twenty-seven years; photograph taken by Francis Gevrier Guittard III.   20

Frank Guittard, Baylor University Academy faculty (c. 1902); studio portrait. 27

Guittards (c. 1948) in backyard at 1401 South 8ᵗʰ Street, Waco. 28

Mamie Welhausen Guittard (c. 1910); age thirty years. 29

Charles Welhausen Guittard (c. 1916); studio portrait, age one year. 30

Francis Gevrier Guittard, Jr. (c. 1922) performing a handstand, age 15 years. 31

Clarence Alwin Guittard (c. 1923), holding white cat. 32

Francis Gevrier Guittard, Jr. (c. 1924); studio portrait. 32

Josie Glenn Guittard (c. 1923); age thirty-eight years; studio portrait. 33

Frank Guittard (c.1926); studio portrait; age fifty-nine. 1

Frank Guittard (c.1932) in Ph.D. gown and mortar board; studio portrait; age sixty-five years. 21

Frank and Josie Guittard's home (c. 1940) at 1401 South 8ᵗʰ Street, Waco. 34

Frank Guittard (c.1948) at his desk in his study at 1401 South 8ᵗʰ Street. 35

Charles Francis Guittard (c.1962) with portrait of Frank Guittard. 36

Photographed handwriting exemplars for the Guittards from the family correspondence collection:

Frank Guittard letter dated June 6, 1920 to Josie Glenn. 38

Frank Guittard letter dated June 20, 1923 to Josie Glenn Guittard. 40

Frank Guittard letter dated June 24, 1926 to Josie Glenn Guittard. 41

Frank Guittard letter dated May 23, 1928 to Josie Glenn Guittard. 42

Frank Guittard letter dated August 11, 1929 to Clarence Alwin Guittard. 43

Josie Glenn Guittard letter dated January 14, 1920 to Frank Guittard. 44

Francis Gevrier Guittard, Jr. letter dated August 19, 1925 to "Folks." 46

Clarence Alwin Guittard letter dated July 23, 1923 to Frank Guittard. 48

Photographic images relating to Baylor University listed immediately below are all courtesy of The Texas Collection, Baylor University, Waco, Texas:

Rufus C. (Columbus) Burleson (c. 1896). 322

Baylor student body (c. 1896), outside Main Building with President Rufus C. Burleson. 323

O. H. (Oscar Henry) Cooper (c. 1899).   324

F. L. (Francis Lafayette) Carroll (c. 1902).   324

G. W. (George Washington) Carroll (c. 1902).   324

Samuel Palmer Brooks (c. 1903).   324

Samuel Palmer Brooks (c. 1923).   325

Georgia Burleson Hall (c. 1896), Baylor University, Burleson Quadrangle, Waco, Texas; Main Building in background.   326

Maggie Houston Hall (c. 1902), on South 5th Street, Waco, Texas.   326

Main Building (c. 1919), Burleson Quadrangle, Waco, Texas.   327

Georgia Burleson Hall (c. 1919), Burleson Quadrangle, Waco, Texas.   328

Photographs relating to Leland Stanford Junior University:

Edgar Eugene Robinson, Ph.D. (c. 1923), Frank Guittard's thesis adviser (1928-1930). Permission from the Stanford Historical Photograph Collection.

329

David Starr Jordan, Ph.D. (c. 1923), President Emeritus of Leland Stanford Junior University. Permission from *The Stanford Daily* and *The 1926 Stanford Quad*.

330

Aerial view of Leland Stanford Junior University (c. 1923). Permission from *The Stanford Daily* and *The 1924 Stanford Quad*.   331

A Ph.D.'s Reverie

Hard times in Ohio,
A train ride to Texas,
A late night in Palo Alto

A Biographical Poem with Historical Notes
About Francis Gevrier Guittard by Charles Francis Guittard

Written by
Charles Francis Guittard

Illustrated by
Grace Elizabeth Daniel

1

Stanford Commencement, June 1931,
A reporter asked the robed figure,
"Dr. Guittard, a moment please,
Now that you have your Ph.D.,
Do you intend to retire?"
A grey-headed Frank faced the young man,
His mind turning without thinking
To the real beginning of his story
Forty-five years before in rural Ohio,

And the memory of a mother
Who hated cold weather,
That terrible storm April of '86,
And loved flowers and growing things…

A brisk September of '86,
Following April's cruel storm,
A year of hard times all around,
Found Frank's family looking southward.
From New Bedford, Ohio
To Chester, Texas was the plan.

Frank, nineteen and restless,
Would scout land for a family move.
Maybe Texas would be the place
For his father to make a new stand,

Buy a farm, hope for a stream of patients new,
More coin of the realm this time,
Less farmers' produce.

He said his goodbyes with his mother--
"God bless you Frank, we'll miss you,
I'll be glad to learn you've done
Something of note in Texas.
Please be sure and write, won't you?"
Those mother's last words so sincerely offered,
All the same, were disturbing to Frank.
He had thought the plan was to return home
After reporting on climate, crops, and prices per acre,
Apparent miscommunication between parents and son.

Were they expecting him to remain in Texas?
It seemed so.
Would he see his family again?
If so, when?
He knew not.
His future would just have to play out in time,
Whether by Providence's inscrutable plan
Or by winds of chance tossing him who knows where.

He grabbed his bag and heaved it onto the rig.
His father urged his best horse and buggy along the path.
They mostly kept their thoughts to themselves
As they passed neighbors' fields and barns,
Voicing only an occasional pleasantry.

At the station after their long ride, an awkward handshake
And final moment between father and son,
The urge to embrace suppressed,
Enough words said the night before,
Nothing more needed for memory's sake.

Now aboard the Pennsylvania Railroad,
Clickety clack, clickety clickety clack, clickety clack,
With a sack of sandwiches, a jug of apple cider,
A few dollars in his pocket, a train schedule,
A dime western or two, a Bible for instruction;
For mind's improvement several volumes
From his father's library—*A Pilgrim's Progress*,
Don Quixote, Gibbon's *Decline and Fall*,—
There would be time to study on the train

During a three-day ride to barely charted land;
A clean shirt, a hat, all packed neatly away,
And a letter of introduction from his father,
In his customary painstaking hand,
Asking for kindly assistance for his son Frank
From any Christian he might meet on his way.

Frank had hoped for a college degree,
His life's central goal,
Someday, somewhere, somehow,
No help would come from home, however,
He knew he was out there on his own.
He felt a little like one of those storied orphans
Who were put on trains to distant States,
They might like their new families,
Or then they might not,
But never to see their poor mothers again.

Two years later he learned without warning
His mother had left this world, the cause uncertain.
He sobbed heartrendingly,
grief and remorse welling up inside,
Never to see his mother again after leaving her that day.
Some things he should have said before he said goodbye
He blamed himself for, some words of appreciation
Never offered, perhaps an apology--
No one will ever know what it was, for Frank never said.

Forty years afterward, in dimly-lit stacks in Palo Alto,
On one of those warm August nights shortly before ten,
After a long day's work making notes in his notebooks,
Scores of dusty volumes still piled high on the table,

An exhausted Frank struggled to stay awake,
His chin occasionally touching his chest, then snapping up.

Suddenly he thought he saw her face near him,
And desperately motioning her to stay
Lest the apparition disappear from view,
Released the feelings he had long wanted to say--
"I hope I've done something to please you, Mother,
Something which may be 'of note'..."

Yet before the apparition could respond,
The Tower Clock began chiming Westminster,
Then gonged ten times, startling Frank awake,
The figure in his dream a memory indelible.

He slowly packed his notebooks, pens, and ink in his case
And walked to the rooming house where he slept.
The concerns of his day were now far away,
In their place a strange peacefulness.

Frank gazed across the Quad
At Mrs. Stanford's Memorial Church,
Listening to the Tower Clock behind the church
Again complete its familiar chimes.
Frank looked down at the reporter,
Answering the lingering question
In his measured manner of speaking,
"No sir"---"Now I'm prepared
To go to work in earnest."
The reporter smiled at the new Ph.D.

The next day, for one last time,
He boarded the Southern Pacific for Texas,
Headed home to Josie, to Waco, and new students.
He would teach "in earnest" into his 84th year
As Baylor's oldest active faculty member.

HISTORICAL NOTES ON THE POEM

Frank's parents:
Dr. Francis Joseph Guittard and Lydia Myers Guittard

Francis ("Frank") Gevrier Guittard, born January 7, 1867, took the train from Ohio to Texas in September 1886 five months after a massive snowstorm and during a nationwide depression affecting his community and his father's medical practice. Dr. F. J. Guittard's practice was the primary support of a large family and his farmer patients were hard-pressed to pay for his services during this period. It was at this time Frank and his parents determined that Frank would scout land for the family in Texas. However, although Frank's subsequent reports back home were generally positive, his father decided he was too old at fifty-nine to start over in Texas. Frank, however, had developed a taste for the new land and decided to stay on rather than return to Ohio.

Frank's mother Lydia died two years after Frank left for Texas, leaving Frank distraught and remorseful although the complete basis for his feelings is not known. We do know that he had been putting off returning home and had not seen her since leaving for Texas.

Guittard Ohio homestead c. 1898 showing Dr. F. J. Guittard standing at far left and Francis Gevrier Guittard ("Frank") sitting to the right looking back towards Dr. F. J. Guittard.

Frank Guittard as Baylor student c. 1894

After two years at Baylor University in Waco and after a total of fifteen years working his way through college, he received his bachelor's degree from the University of Chicago in 1901 and a master's from Chicago in 1902. In 1902 following a stranger than fiction twist of fate in which Baylor President Oscar Cooper was provoked to throw a small dog out a third-story chapel window, Frank accepted an offer from newly installed Baylor President Samuel P. Brooks to teach in Baylor's Preparatory Department in Waco. Frank and Brooks had known each other since their Baylor days. Then twenty-one years later at age fifty-six, Chair of Baylor's History Department since 1910, and grand marshal of Baylor commencements for years, he commenced Ph.D. studies at Stanford, attending mostly in the summers. He received his doctorate in 1931 at age 64. Thereafter, he taught at Baylor into his 84th year and was still teaching history when he died in Dallas. A historian who was a secret romantic, he had gone to see Donizetti's *L'elisir d'amore* (*The Elixir of Love*) at the Dallas opera but was stricken before the opening curtain.

Mamie Welhausen, Frank's first wife and the mother of all his children, died in 1917 of tuberculosis at age thirty-seven. Josie Glenn, or "Mama Josie", was Frank's second wife who survived him. Frank was also survived by Francis Jr. born in 1907 and Clarence born in 1917, both of whom obtained their college education in four years or less and became attorneys. A son Charles died in infancy in 1916.

Dr. Samuel P. Brooks, Baylor's President during 1902-1931 and a graduate of both Baylor and Yale University, wanted all department chairs to have doctorates and made that clear frequently. Frank's pursuit of a Ph.D. in history as an older student who was married with children, was a long one and mostly lonely and grueling; however, once his Ph.D. was in hand, he returned to Baylor re-energized and taught history another nineteen years.

Dr. Edgar E. Robinson, later Chair of Stanford's History Department, directed Frank Guittard's Ph.D. dissertation. He was twenty years younger than Frank and born in 1887.

With the exception of Frank's encounter with an apparition in the library, the poem is largely biographical and most of the details, including the conversation with the reporter, are based on written records. "Going to work in earnest" was one of Frank's best known expressions. The titles of classic written works shown in two of the illustrations were books in his father's library which Frank recorded he read.

The Tower Clock, originally part of Memorial Church, at all relevant times during Frank's studies at Stanford resided in temporary quarters inside a wooden tower behind Memorial Church which had sustained serious damage during the 1906 earthquake. The use of a pocket watch shown in several of the later illustrations evidences a life-long theme: that Frank felt from the day he left Ohio that he was running against the clock where obtaining his college education was concerned; later his conspicuous pocket watch would be one of Frank's trademarks as a teacher.

Pocket watch Frank Guittard won in 1894
as a summer book salesman

If Frank did see his mother's face during his work on his Ph.D. at Stanford, he kept it to himself. However, there can be no doubt that his mother had a profound influence on him and that during his days in residence at Palo Alto, he had a lot of time to reflect on the path his life had taken, including his separation from her and the rest of his Ohio family, for the most part from September 1886 on.

Some 200,000 orphans and neglected children were relocated by the Children's Aid Society from the 1860's through the 1920's commonly using trains. Frank was neither a child, an orphan, nor a neglected child. His large Ohio family with seven surviving children was caught by the depression of the times when difficult decisions sometimes had to be made.

Frank in Ph.D. gown and mortar board in 1932

COLLEGE ESSAY,
BAYLOR UNIVERSITY, 1894

Essay, Narrative and Instructional
Spring 1894, F. G. Guittard
Class: The Giant Rhetoric Class
Teacher: W. W. Franklin
Preparation time: fourteen hours [hand-written]

THE CARAVAN ACROSS THE LAND OF TOIL*

In the autumnal month of September 1893, a caravan was to start from IGNORANCE, one of the most populous cities on the face of the earth, and make a journey across a region of country quite generally known as the LAND of TOIL. Let us view the company as they are making their final preparations for travel. They have come outside the walls of the city and are assembled on the PLAIN of HOPE which extends north of it. The pilgrims hail from different parts of the world. There is about an equal number of both sexes in the company. Were you to ask each one what their object is in making the journey, you would discover that some have a very indefinite idea of the real purpose of this undertaking, while others have some noble aim in view.

There are quite a number of important personages in this band of travelers. The most distinguished looking man in the crowd is the guide, ABOU BEN ENERGY, an Arab who has conducted many caravans across the LAND of TOIL. He is mounted on a large, one-humped, ill-natured camel. Those who have traveled with this noted guide, know his faithful animal as OLD CRITICISM. Although he is such an unsightly looking creature, yet he has many valuable qualities. His speed and power of endurance are remarkable. He truly deserves to be called the "ship of the desert." The force of his kicks are terrible to be experienced and...to be witnessed. Several ugly scars are noticeable on his back and sides. These show that OLD CRITICISM and his master have been in some desperate conflicts in their travels.

Next to the guide in prominence, is Mr. PROMPTNESS, who is mounted on a high-spirited steed named GET-UP-and-GET. The young lady who...so gracefully is Miss PUNCTUALITY. By her side rides Miss NEATNESS, on a cream-colored donkey named PRUDENCE. That is Seignior ACCURACY on the dromedary. The last in the line are Mr. BEHIND-TIME mounted on the personification of contumacy, and Miss UNREADY riding a Texas mustang she calls DON'T-CARE. In all, there are sixty in the company, each one mounted and equipped for the journey.

The caravan is now ready to start. Abou Ben addresses them: He says: Fellow travelers, you have a long and difficult journey before you. There will be deserts to cross as well as mountains to climb. O[h], what weary nights of privation you shall go through! I will not speak of those who have attempted to cross this country and have turned back in despair, nor of those who were not able to keep up with the company in which they started and were hopelessly lost. Let us look at the other side. Those who have completed this journey have been repaid one hundred fold for the privations and difficulties they endured. Although desert regions are to be traversed, yet there are many delightful oases in them where are to be found the most beautiful flowers, delicious fruits, and bubling [sic] fountains of clear sparkling water. Here you may rest in the cool shade of tropical trees after your weary travel. When climbing the hills and mountains, you will [find] precious stones, such as the opal, emerald, and diamond and may even [find] nuggets of silver and gold.

The first city we shall come to by and by in the LAND of TOIL is KNOWLEDGE and in the prosperous country of SUCCESS. The other important [cities] of this country are HONOR, FAME, PLEASURE, WEALTH, and CONTENTMENT. These cities are a great distance apart and it requires years of travel to reach them even after coming to knowledge. It is most important to reach the latter place. And in order for you to do this I wish to impress upon you the necessity of doing your duty. *Remember that system conquers all things and that a reward awaits all who are loyal to duty.**

The guide now gives the signal and the caravan starts off. They travel several weeks without any serious trouble. They camp on alternate days during the week and sometimes have a feast. After breaking up camp, each member of the company is allowed to pursue his own investigations along the way, but must follow the directions the guide gives. The guide announces to the company at the end of this time that the next camping place would be on the oasis called FOOD. After some hard travel the palm trees are seen in the distance, rising above the horizon. Mr. PROMPTITUDE and Miss PUNCTUALITY are the first to reach the oasis, the remainder of the company except one or two are close behind. Miss UNREADY, Mr. BEHIND-TIME and Father PROCRASTINATION came in the next day. The guide has been somewhat impatient about the delay. OLD CRITICISM has been attempting to break loose from his master. He has succeeded in getting loose without much effort and comes right toward the crowd. All are in suspense. Mr. CURLYCUE is the first to suffer. He receives a kick from the left hind foot of OLD CRITICISM that renders him sprawling to the ground. The raging animal is no respecter of persons and all come in contact with him before he is checked in his mad _____ by his master. From this place the company travel on and reach many other pleasant places, but not without some weary labor.

The company have now been on the journey seven months. They have met with all kinds of difficulties and deserts. They have withstood_____, _____, and

Hurricanes, but now an ALLIGORY [sic] strikes the caravan with the terrible force all but a few of the company were buried in the sand. Those who escaped the storm are said to have reached the CITY OF KNOWLEDGE. And afterward to have taken up their abode in the different cities of the LAND of SUCCESS.

*[Editor's note: *This hand-written essay by Frank Guittard was completed during his last term at Baylor University at the end of his second year before his lack of funds forced him to drop out. The work was untitled. The editor has taken the liberty of supplying a title intended to capture the spirit of the essay. The essay itself was actually written in a style of cursive script closely resembling the widely-used Spencerian script. Examples of Frank's handwriting can be seen in the exemplars of his letters included in this work. In a few instances where the editor could not read a word in the copy he had, he left a blank space, and in others, made his best approximation of the word.*

One may suppose the name of the caravan guide "Abou Ben Energy" could have been inspired by the classic poem "Abou Ben Adhem" by Leigh Hunt which Frank possibly read for an English class at Baylor. Of course, the theme of the essay somewhat resembles that of John Bunyan's allegory, A Pilgrim's Progress, which there is reason to believe had been in his father's library in Ohio.

One line above has been italicized by the editor to emphasize the apparent moral of the essay ("Remember that system conquers all things and that a reward awaits all who are loyal to duty..."). Frank's letters to his family contained infra show his devotion to system and to duty. However, the letters also underscore his belief, developed from painful experience obtained in the next three decades after leaving Baylor, in the importance of starting the caravan off in the correct direction, with careful individual preparation, sufficient resources, and a plan to meet any contingency--subjects not directly addressed in the 1894 essay.]

Portraits, Photographs, and Snapshots

The Guittard Family

Francis Gevrier Guittard [studio portrait, c. 1902); Baylor University
Academy faculty

Guittards (c.1948) in backyard at 1401 South 8th; Frank Guittard on the back row at left holding his hat with Francis Guittard, Clarence Guittard, and Dixie Lynn Guittard to his left; on the front row, Philip Guittard, John Guittard, Charles Guittard, Stephen Guittard, and Josie Guittard at the far right.

Mamie Welhausen Guittard
(c. 1910);
age thirty years.

Charles Welhausen Guittard (c. 1916);
studio portrait, age one year.

Francis Gevrier Guittard, Jr. (c. 1922)
performing a handstand, age fifteen years.

Clarence Alwin Guittard (c. 1923),
holding white cat.

Francis Gevrier Guittard, Jr. (c.1924).

Josie Glenn Guittard (c. 1923).

Frank and Josie Guittard's home (c. 1940)
at 1401 South 8th Street, Waco.

Frank Guittard (c.1948)
at his desk in his study at 1401 South 8th Street.

Charles Francis Guittard (c.1962)
with portrait of Frank Guittard.

Handwriting Exemplars

for the
Guittard Correspondence

Frank Guittard letter dated June 6, 1920 to Josie Glenn.

My dearest Josie,

I do not know whether this letter will get to you Wed or Thurs. Francis and I were invited out for supper and as it happened just as we were ready to go into the dining room some callers came so I was rather late getting back home

I have been moving around pretty briskly this afternoon getting the programs in shape so that I will not have so much to do when I come back with my bride or I am afraid she will feel neglected.

I went for the ring this afternoon also. It is all complete and I hope you will like it.

Some very cordial congratulations have been

Frank Guittard letter dated June 6, 1920 to Josie Glenn(continued).

offered here and there as I have
been moving around. Most of
them really seem to mean what
they say.

I have forty little
chicks but Francis will know
how to manage them. We
have been enjoying roasting ears
the past few days from the garden.

This is the last letter I shall
write to my sweetheart. That does
not mean however that we shall
cease to be sweethearts. I hope
as the years go by we shall
continue to be sweethearts and
that our love for each other
will grow as the years
pass. Until I see you
With devoted love
Frank

Tuesday

Frank Guittard letter dated June 20, 1923
to Josie Glenn Guittard.

Baylor University
Waco, Texas

DEPARTMENT OF HISTORY
FRANCIS GEVINER GUITTARD, A. M.
RESIDENCE
1401 SOUTH 8TH STREET

Stanford Uni.
Calif.
6-20-23
Before breakfast

Dearest Josie,

I went through the red tape of registration yesterday. They have the details all worked out to a fine point. Even had my picture taken as one of the steps in the registration. Immense is the best word to describe the University. I am writing again this morning for I get so deeply involved after today that may not have much leisure. I was awfully glad I arrived for registration day. Your letter was awaiting me. It made me feel just a little homesick and wonder just why I was way out here for etc. I am sending some checks for you to deposit at the Citizens National. I think I have enough to run me for the summer.

With love to all
Frank.

Frank Guittard letter dated June 24, 1926
to Josie Glenn Guittard.

FRANCIS GEVRIER GUITTARD, A.M.
RESIDENCE: 1401 SOUTH 5TH STREET

Baylor University
Department of History
Waco, Texas

Stanford U.
6-24-26

Dearest Josie,

I am in the midst of it again and going finely. I wish you would send me by Parcel Post Hulme's History of the British People. I think you will find it in the History office at the University. Also send Beasley, Forbes, Birkett, Russia from the Varangian to the Bolsheviki. You will find this among the other books. If you don't find it send Platonof or Platonov - Russia, but I would rather have Beasley etc's book. Have been meeting a few of my old student friends, among them Smith from Idaho, the Mormon. Have a dandy room, no flies, no roommate, Love Frank

Box 2437

41

Frank Guittard letter dated May 23, 1928 to Josie Guittard.

Frank Guittard letter dated August 11, 1929
to Clarence Alwin Guittard.

> Sun, Aug 11, 1929
>
> Dear Clarence;
>
> You should have put up a better fight when those girls got after you.
>
> How are your pet roses getting on? How are things looking around the place? Tell me all about something. See whether you can write me a a story of three or four or five or six pages on something you have been doing or would like to do.
>
> Tell Mama Josie that the plan suggested in her letter suits me all right. Just let me know when "you all" will be at Albuquerque and where and I will try to make connection as near as possible,
>
> With love
> Papa.

Josie Glenn Guittard letter dated January 14, 1920
to Frank Guittard.

Josie Glenn letter dated January 14, 1920 to Frank Guittard (continued)

Francis Gevrier Guittard, Jr. letter dated August 19, 1925 to "Folks."

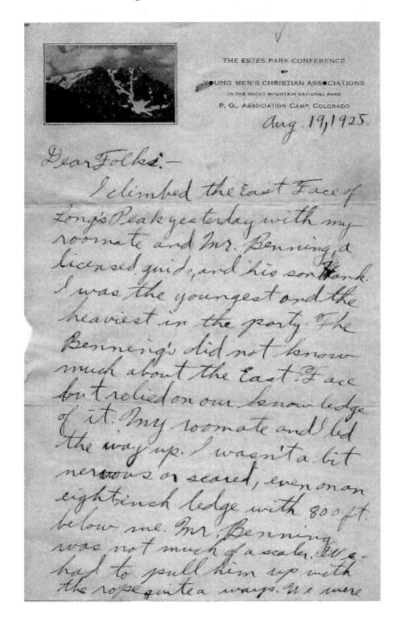

THE ESTES PARK CONFERENCE
OF
YOUNG MEN'S CHRISTIAN ASSOCIATIONS
IN THE ROCKY MOUNTAIN NATIONAL PARK
P. O., ASSOCIATION CAMP, COLORADO

Aug. 19, 1925.

Dear Folks:—

I climbed the East Face of Long's Peak yesterday with my roomate and Mr. Benning, a licensed guide, and his son Frank. I was the youngest and the heaviest in the party. The Benning's did not know much about the East Face but relied on our knowledge of it. My roomate and I led the way up. I wasn't a bit nervous or scared, even on an eight-inch ledge with 800 ft. below me. Mr. Benning was not much of a scaler. We had to pull him up with the rope quite a ways. We were

Francis Gevrier Guittard, Jr. letter dated August 19, 1925 to "Folks," (continued)

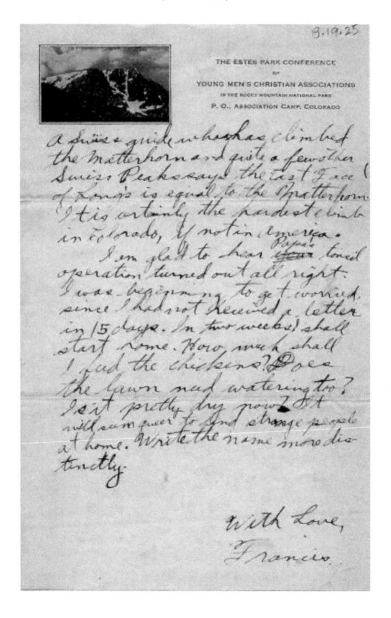

Clarence Alwin Guittard letter dated July 23, 1923
to Frank Guittard.

THE LETTERS
THE "COURTSHIP LETTERS"
(1920-1922)
THE "PALO ALTO LETTERS"
(1923-1930)

The Letters

The "Courtship Letters"
(1920-1922)

The "Palo Alto Letters"
(1923-1930)

Frank Guittard was a widower with two young sons when he and Josie Glenn, a Houston school teacher, were married on June 10, 1920, after a whirlwind "won't take no for an answer" courtship conducted mostly by letter. The courtship began in December 1919 after the two were introduced by Judge and Mrs. Thomas F. Bryan (Tom and Katherine) at First Baptist Church in Waco while Josie was visiting the Bryans in Waco, likely during the Christmas holidays. Josie generally referred to them as "cousins." Judge Bryan was an attorney, a federal referee in bankruptcy, and at one time, a judge in the Corporation Court of Waco.

Frank had previously married the late Mamie Welhausen Guittard in 1906 in Shiner, Texas. They had three sons, two surviving as of Frank's second marriage to Josie: Francis Gevrier Guittard, Jr. ("Francis," age thirteen) and Clarence Alwin Guittard ("Clarence," age three, sometimes called "Sonny Boy"). Clarence had been separated from his mother Mamie at barely a month old, when she was sent to a tuberculosis sanatorium in Albuquerque, New Mexico. Mamie died less than a month later after all attempts to prolong her life proved futile. Frank had placed Clarence in the care of his elderly mother-in-law Eliza Amsler Welhausen in Shiner with the primary day-to-day care-taking falling to a family friend, Mrs. Mewes, whom Clarence affectionately referred to as "Auntie Mama."

The early letters between Frank and Josie prior to the Palo Alto period letters are referred to for convenience as "The Courtship Letters," namely those between January 1920 and September 1922 that were exchanged while Frank was in Waco (one letter from Frank existing) and Josie in Houston. Josie, who had never been married, was a thirty-seven-year-old school teacher and the eldest child from a farming family in Bronte, Texas. At the time of their marriage, Frank had earned two degrees, including a master's from the University of Chicago, and was chair of Baylor University's History Department. Josie must have had either some years of college or a certificate from a state normal school, allowing her to teach in Texas public schools. However, Frank and Josie were both strong Baptists, shared many cultural interests, and came from large farming families, Frank in Ohio and Josie in Texas. Although in appearance they were strikingly different, Josie being short and stout, and Frank being tall, somewhat stout and eighteen years her senior, they were remarkably compatible in most facets of marriage.

"The Palo Alto Letters" refers to the family letters, beginning with Frank's first summer attending Stanford University as a student in residence in 1923 through his final summer in 1930. Frank's letters were mostly written in Palo Alto; Josie's mostly in Waco. Family letters from 1924 and 1925, when Frank was not in residence, and one letter from September 1930 after his Ph.D. work was concluded but before he had received his degree, are also included for continuity and a sense of completeness. Frank's six periods in residence in Palo Alto (or Stanford) were:

June-August 1923
June-August 1926
June-August 1927
January-August 1928
June-August 1929
June-August 1930

While a student at Stanford, Frank changed his residence several times, sometimes rooming in a dormitory, usually staying in a rooming house off campus in Palo Alto, but always rooming alone so that he could use the room as a quiet study and workplace when not in class or the library. Frank did not generally take meals where he lived, but preferred to eat at restaurants and cafeterias including the Union cafeteria on the Stanford campus. Wherever he roomed, the accommodation would have been vastly superior to that he experienced as a freshman at Baylor's Maggie Houston Hall in 1890. Maggie, a dormitory owned by Baylor available to male students who could not afford a private boarding house, offered rooms with wood-burning stoves and double-beds, but without electric light or indoor plumbing.

He received his doctoral sheepskin at Stanford's commencement on June 16, 1931 after a total of twenty-three months in residence. Baylor University President Samuel Palmer Brooks, who had insisted that all Baylor department chairs should have Ph.D.s, died May 14, 1931. We suspect, however, that President Brooks had already thanked Frank for the completion of his Ph.D. work, which Frank finished up in August 1930.

The context for these two groups of handwritten letters—The Courtship Letters and The Palo Alto Letters—included a number of controversies roiling the waters during the period 1920-1930 that were impacting Baylor, its faculty, students, and supporters, who were overwhelmingly Baptists. Perhaps the most important was the evolution controversy stemming from the 1859 publication of Charles Darwin's *Origin of the Species,* which reached the Baylor campus sixty years later. This tsunami of controversy over evolution and the teaching of evolution theory engulfed Baylor and the Southern Baptist denomination, to one extent or another, and other universities, as well as seminaries, throughout the 1920s. Frank at the time was focused, on the one hand, on preparing for and teaching his classes, and, on the other hand, establishing a marital relationship with Josie (June 1920), bringing three-year-old Clarence home to Waco (May 1921), and then commencing Ph.D. studies at Stanford (1923). However, that tsunami was already in evidence and gathering force even before Frank married Josie and certainly years before he left for Palo Alto in 1923.

The editor's notes infra develop the challenges that President Brooks and Baylor were facing in the 1920s, short-term and long-term, including, but not limited to, the dispute over the proposal to relocate Baylor from Waco to Dallas (a short-term dispute) and the evolution controversy at Baylor (a controversy lasting a decade), incidents of which are set out below following the words, "Editor's note on President Brooks' battles:." One caveat should be noted: the intent herein is to suggest chronologically some, but not all, of the incidents relating to these matters so as to show what was going on generally behind the scenes in the lives of the Guittards, not to show them in any detail. That must be left to the scholars on these subjects.

Other important controversies affecting Baylor during the 1920s occurred as well, but those are stories reserved for *The Life & Times of Frank Guittard,* except only to say that Frank played an important role in connection with the rise and fall of Baylor's Student Self-Government Association.

The chief characters in the letters, the editor's notes to the letters, and the Epilogue are Frank Guittard, Josie "Mama Josie" Glenn Guittard, Francis Gevrier Guittard, Jr., Clarence ("Sonny boy") Alwin Guittard, Baylor President Brooks, and Edgar Eugene Robinson, Ph.D. (Frank's dissertation adviser). The editor's notes and the Epilogue include a number of additional characters who played roles in the evolution controversy subtheme for the years Frank Guittard spent pursuing his Ph.D., among them being U.S. politician and presidential candidate William Jennings Bryan, Reverend John Roach Straton, Reverend William Bell Riley, and Reverend J. Frank Norris, an alumnus of Baylor.

The Courtship Letters of Frank and Josie

Following chronologically below are excerpts from all the surviving courtship letters of Frank and Josie. Considering that Frank made his mind up very quickly about Josie and was suggesting marriage almost at the outset of their relationship, it is probable that he wrote at least as many letters to her as she did to him. Possibly his letters to her were longer since he was ardently trying to make a case for himself and for joining his little family in Waco, she initially remaining cautiously stand-offish. Although only one letter of his survives from this period, the content of the missing letters may be safely inferred from Josie's letters.

January 6, 1920 (Tuesday)

Dear Mr. Guittard,

Arrived in Houston Sunday morning. Went out to the boarding house where I have been for some years...Have a very nice room, could be a little better, but with living conditions as they are, am sure I should be satisfied.

Was in a Hudson and it is manipulated somewhat differently from the Buick.

Hope you have a pleasant year's work. Well say good night. Write.

Sincerely Josie Glenn.

[Editor's note: It is not clear what Josie was referring to in her remark about "living conditions as they are." Josie was possibly referring to having to share a room with one or more roommates, possibly school teachers like herself.

Ownership of automobiles in the United States had picked up by the 1920s.]

[Editor's note on President Brooks' battles: Just prior to the evolution controversy reaching Baylor in 1920, Reverend William Bell Riley led a World Conference on Christian Fundamentals in Philadelphia in 1919. Riley was the driving force behind the World Christian Fundamentals Association (WCFA) and perhaps the first important voice protesting the teaching of evolution, particularly at church-related or tax-supported schools.

Central to the theological position of the WCFA was the belief in the infallibility of scripture including Genesis, the first book in the Old Testament, and all scriptural passages describing miracles. Baylor's unwitting entrance into the controversy is described below following Josie's April 28, 1920 letter to Frank.]

January 14, 1920 (Wednesday)

Dear Mr. Guittard,

Had your letter a few days ago and I appreciate all the nice things you said but I hardly know how to reply. I like you and would like to be a good friend to you and would like for you to be a good friend to me but beyond that I cannot see...

I have been riding in a Buick once since I have been back, but did not do any of the driving. I do not believe I have forgotten what you taught me...

We are to have a Musical Concert next week and I am planning to go. Shall I hear out of one ear for you?...Well say goodbye.

Sincerely, Josie Glenn.

[Editor's note: Frank and Josie were well-matched, but one major impetus for the whirlwind speed of the courtship was the fact that three-year-old Clarence had been living in Shiner since probably shortly before Mamie's death in May 1917. Frank was eager to bring him back to Waco.]

January 29, 1920 (Thursday)

Dear Mr. Guittard,

I am so sorry you have been sick. You should be careful and stay in when the doctor tells you to because, as you say, colds are very treacherous and you should not take a chance…

Well I am still at a loss as to what to write you for I am not of the same opinion as you are. I wonder if I am wrong in writing at all… Really and truly I do not think we have known each other long enough to be any more than friends. Please let's just be good friends…

How is your garden progressing? Our seasons are some earlier than yours…

I appreciate the nice things you have said. I know you think I am hard headed and I may be just a little bit because I do have ideas of my own.

Bye, bye

Sincerely, Josie Glenn

[Editor's note: The common cold was a topic about which Frank had strong feelings and a detailed program for its avoidance. Colds and other illnesses had always constituted a threat to his staying on track with his goals for his education, not to mention a well-justified concern for the health of his family members. There is more on this topic later in a letter from Frank to Francis and in a letter to Josie from Palo Alto, Frank having lost both his second son Charles and first wife Mamie to infectious disease in 1916 and 1917 respectively.]

February 2, 1920 (Monday)

Dear Mr. Guittard,

It is only ten or twelve minutes ride from the Rice [Hotel] to where I live on the streetcar and I am just two blocks off the South End Streetcar.

Remember I have made no promises concerning your coming down here but if you just want to come to see me I shall be glad to have you come. I know you will look all dressed up in your new suit. I like brown and often wear it…

Mama wrote me the other day that she has ten little chicks, said she has had friers all winter…

Goodbye, Josie Glenn

February 5, 1920 (Thursday)

Dear Mr. Guittard,

I heartily approve of all your avocations. As to the chickens, Mama says you get thriftier chickens from mixed breeds than you do from the pedigreed and she is fairly successful. Her pet chickens are the Rhode Island Reds…

I shall be glad to have you come over if you really would care to come…Good night

Sincerely, Josie Glenn

[Editor's note: Frank, thanks to his experience in Ohio working on the family farm, had some knowledge about various breeds of farm animals, hogs in particular. Both Josie and Frank came from large farming families. Frank kept a chicken coop behind the house on South 8th Street in Waco where he and Josie lived for twenty-nine years and possibly behind the house on South 7th Street before that where he lived with Mamie, his late first wife.

We lack Frank's early letters to Josie, but they probably would have shown that he realized early on that he needed to at least appease Mrs. Glenn, if not make her into an outright supporter of a marriage between him and her daughter. Mrs. Glenn relied on Josie as the oldest child for emotional support, if not financial, and ostensibly had little to gain from Josie marrying a teacher in Waco. Waco was over 170 miles closer to Bronte than Houston, however.]

February 27, 1920 (Friday)

Dear Mr. Guittard,

So I am to see you March 2. Will you arrive in the morning or evening? My telephone is Hadley 4666...I am glad that Baylor is to be made larger by the addition of new departments...

Sincerely, Josie Glenn

[Editor's note: Baylor University saw significant expansion to its professional schools during the 1920s and shortly before. In 1918 the College of Dentistry was created and in 1920 both the School of Law and the School of Nursing. The College of Medicine and the College of Pharmacy had been created as of 1903 and 1904, respectively. The College of Fine Arts and the School of Music were established in 1921. All of these colleges or schools were created during President Brooks' presidency.]

April 8, 1920 (Thursday)

Dear Mr. Guittard,

Since I am just an ordinary human, I fear I cannot live up to all the nice things you say about me. I like and admire you but I don't think I want to get married.... I have thought and thought about what you have said to me, and I am still thinking...

How are your little chicks and the garden. These cold northers are not very helpful to either...

Very glad to hear you are planning to be here for a longer visit the next time....

Most sincerely, Josie Glenn

April 16, 1920 (Friday)

Dear Mr. Guittard,

I am the oldest of a family of nine children...We have one brother dead and we have one sister who taught for two years and her health gave way mentally and physically...Two of my sisters work in the bank at Bronte. My three brothers are in a garage and my baby sister... is in school...My father is a farmer on a small scale. I think my mother is just the bravest somebody I know...

Sincerely, Josie G.

[Editor's note: In some ways, Frank and Josie's backgrounds were similar. Both came from large families where at least part of the family income came from farming. However, Frank's father had a medical degree, a medical practice, and most of his children were able to attend some college, with two becoming physicians. No information is available as to what happened to Josie's sister.]

April 18, 1920 (Sunday)

Dearest Frank,

My dear, I eat most anything for breakfast. I usually eat some fruit, an egg and bacon and toast. Whatever you want Fannie to prepare will please me...

With lots and lots of love to you and to Francis, Josie.

[Editor's note: Having a hearty appetite was also something Frank and Josie had in common, neither being especially thin in 1920 or afterwards.]

April 19, 1920 (Monday)

Dear Mr. Guittard,

Had your letter today and I am glad you are to be in Houston Friday....Do you remember that my telephone number is Hadley 4666?

Well say goodnight and see you Friday.

Sincerely, Josie Glenn

_____, 1920 (day of week and month unknown)

[Dear Frank]

Had a nice letter from Mama today. She said if I wanted to get married it was all right with her. I knew she would not be very enthusiastic because she has never encouraged our getting married…

One week from today you will be here…

Devotedly, proudly, Josie.

[Editor's note: It is not clear whether Josie, in mentioning her mother's lack of enthusiasm for marriage, is talking about Josie and Frank getting married to each other, or Josie or any of her brothers and sisters getting married to anyone. It is possibly the former, as Josie was the eldest child and a source of emotional support for Mrs. Glenn. Since the day of week and month are unknown, placement of this letter here in the chronology represents a best guess.]

April 28, 1920 (Wednesday)

Dearest Frank,

It will be my pleasure and happiness.... with you and your boys [to] make our home a real home. The tenth of June will suit me perfectly...Just now I have to plan clothes because I want you never to be ashamed of me....Write to me soon because I love to get your letters.

Lots and lots of love, Josie.

[Editor's note on President Brooks' battles: Shortly after the above letter, in May 1920 Baylor unknowingly ignited an evolution controversy in Waco when it published Professor Grove Samuel Dow's Principles of Sociology, Dow at the time being chair of the Baylor Sociology Department. Dow's textbook contained a number of sentences regarding the age and first appearance of the human species that were at odds in the minds of some Christians with the first chapter of Genesis. These sentences sparked a controversy involving Baylor that would last from 1920 through 1930 and afterward.

J. Frank Norris, a Baylor graduate, and other fundamentalist preachers, carried out scathing attacks on Baylor and Baylor President Brooks as part of a broad-based holy war waged by many fundamentalists across the U.S. that pitted Baptists against Baptists and members of other Christian denominations against each other.

One student at Baylor during the early 1920s said in an interview with the editor that the campus was permeated by the evolution controversy between 1920 and 1924. At that time the Baylor community had not likely seen a controversy with that much heat since the brilliant master of journalistic invective William Cowper Brann in the mid-1890s, for whom the truth was never really the only point, savagely attacked Baylor and President Rufus C. Burleson in his publication The Iconoclast. Brann, whose Iconoclast at one time had a circulation of 100,000 readers, had asserted that President Burleson had shielded a sexual predator and covered up a crime, which assertion was vigorously denied by President Burleson and his supporters. It was not long afterward that Brann, who was almost lynched by a group of angry Baylor students, was fatally shot in the back in a shoot-out on the streets of downtown Waco. However, after taking the bullet which eventually killed him, he was nevertheless able to draw his Colt revolver and dispatch his assassin.]

June 8, 1920 (Tuesday)

My dearest Josie,

I do not know whether this letter will get to you Wednesday or Thursday...I have been moving around pretty briskly this afternoon getting the programs in shape so that I will not have so much to do when I come back with my bride or I am afraid she will feel neglected.

I went for the ring this afternoon also. It is all complete and I hope you will like it...

I have forty little chicks but Francis will know how to manage them. We have been enjoying roasting ears the past few days from the garden....Until I see you.

With devoted love, Frank

[Editor's note: The "programs" were likely history courses Frank was teaching at Baylor. Frank's farming background and avocation is also evident.]

[Editor's note on President Brooks' battles: President Brooks believed that the evolution controversy reached Baylor when evangelist T.T. Martin in 1921 complained about several paragraphs in Baylor Professor Grove Samuel Dow's The Principles of Sociology. The subsequent attacks on Baylor by J. Frank Norris, pastor of First Baptist Church in Fort Worth, all made a similar complaint.

Thereafter, Professor Dow decided to resign in December 1921. Norris attacked President Brooks for allowing infidelity and heresy among Baylor faculty and Brooks issued a denial of the heresy charge. Norris began a rancorous campaign against Baylor University and a personal attack on President Brooks in 1921 for teaching evolution and heresy which lasted for ten or more years.

In early 1922 Brooks suggested that Southern Baptists investigate and resolve the charges against Baylor, and thus a questionnaire was distributed to determine whether evolution was being taught or advocated at Baptist colleges.

In September, just after the next letter below, the Baptist Standard published the investigating committee's report, which supported Baylor's defense against the charges of Norris and others.]

August 29, 1922 (Tuesday)

Dearest Josie,

A letter came this morning came from Miss [name of renter] saying that her cousin here in the city wishes her to stay with her in the winter so that leaves one vacancy. I suppose it will be all right if a good looking school marm is in need of shelter to take her in.

We are having fine cool nights since the rain. Hope you found all well.

Lovingly, Frank

September 3, 1922 (Sunday)

Dear Sweetheart,

I am afraid you will think you have a very reckless husband if I tell you something. Well, Saturday morning I decided to do something extremely daring. I invited the Bryans to dinner with me Sunday. After some diplomatic negotiations my proposition was accepted. It was "up to me." I "hotfooted" it to the pigley wigley and loaded up with cabbage, lettuce and carrots as well as fruits and other embellishments. There is one less Rhode Islander striding about in the backyard. He was transformed into a smothered chicken. Then also there is one less bottle of grape juice on the pantry shelf. It was "transfrigerated" into sherbet excellent'.

The Judge [Tom Bryan] and his lady arrived in good time after a fine sermon at church. Conversation was soon cut short by the silvery tinkle of the bell and host and guests *marcharon'* to the table. When preliminaries were over operations began in earnest. There was a spirited attack from three sides in harmonious action. The smothered fowl was complimented as well as the salad which was the prescribed combination of cabbage and carrots...Mariah had persuaded the sausage grinder to negotiate the ingredients. The sherbet was fine and not at all slighted even in the absence of Francis. It had some cake to accompany it and relieve the situation when the sherbet got too cold. It did have a strong tendency to remove all the heat from store-bought teeth as was remarked from the side opposite the host [possibly Judge Bryan].

The guests seemed to be thinking that the feast was over ...when the door swung aside and the waitress appeared with dignified and stately tread carrying a tray with three glasses and some "old time democracy." One time at least we were all together on the political platform...

Tell Clarence his tricycle looks neglected and out of humor in the back hall and that Teddy on the davenport sticks up his nose every time I pass him...

Lovingly, Frank

[Editor's notes: Frank's "pigley wigley" is misspelled, perhaps as a joke, or perhaps it was mainly Josie's role to shop at Piggly Wiggly in Waco and Frank rarely saw the signs. The Bryans were members of First Baptist Church in Waco, possibly cousins of Josie, and had introduced Frank and Josie. Frank does not say specifically what "old time democracy" was served on this particular occasion, but Prohibition had been the law of the land since 1919, although it was not always observed in private homes. It appears that he and his guests were unanimous in opposing Prohibition, but may have been on opposite sides on other political issues. There is no way of knowing whether Josie would have shared some of the "old time democracy" had she been present, but we suspect she would have been conflicted on that matter.

This letter is the only record of Frank preparing a meal for invited guests; we conclude that the described occasion was rare and possibly a one-of-a-kind.]

The Palo Alto Letters: Frank, Josie, Francis, and Clarence

Several hundred letters survive from this time period. The ones excerpted below were selected as being representative of the group as a whole.

Following a number of the letters below are editor's notes on President Brooks' battles back in Waco. The years 1923, 1924, and 1925 were momentous years as the attacks on Baylor, President Brooks, and the Baylor faculty were heavy and unrelenting, notwithstanding the favorable report of the investigating committee mentioned above.

In March 1923, a Baylor ministerial student named Dale Crowley complained that history professor Charles S. Fothergill made comments in a European history class supportive of evolution theory and claimed that Fothergill did not believe the story of Noah's Ark found in *Genesis*. Crowley then met separately, both with Fothergill and with President Brooks, to register his complaint about the teaching he claimed he had received.

J. Frank Norris' newspaper *The Searchlight* reported in April that Baylor students had asked President Brooks to resign. At the end of May, Norris came to Waco and spoke to Baylor students at Waco City Auditorium. Baylor, through President Brooks in particular, denied Crowley's charges and the subsequent attacks by Norris and other fundamentalist Baptist preachers, countering that Baylor faculty members did not espouse the theory of evolution in their classes, but appropriately educated students as to the tenets of the theory. In June, Crowley sent out several letters referencing his complaints about Fothergill, Baylor, and President Brooks.

Our only record of Frank Guittard's reaction to the controversy surrounding the allegation against Fothergill is that Frank told his son Clarence that he felt strongly against Norris' attack on a member of his department and that Fothergill was only explaining the theory of evolution. Additionally, we suspect Frank viewed any discussion of Noah's Ark as completely extraneous to, and of no use whatsoever in, teaching European history and that Fothergill had needlessly "stepped in it." Our suspicion is mostly speculative, but primarily based on the obvious fact that there was no real reason to talk about Noah's Ark in teaching history courses.

June 10, 1923 (Sunday)

Dearest Frank,

Am anxious to know how you like Leland Stanford [University] and if you find the work very heavy. Hope you won't find your correspondence work too much along with your other courses. Seems to me that I send you something almost every day. A hug, kiss and goodnight.

Love, Josie

[Editor's note: Through the years Frank had a number of students who took correspondence courses from him requiring written work that he had to grade. He continued this work while in Palo Alto in addition to his Stanford coursework, with Josie mailing him the students' papers for grading.

Clarence said in an interview that Frank kept a box of graded correspondence papers in his library at 1401 South 8th Street in Waco. Clarence was allowed to use old student papers as drawing paper and probably also as materials to make paper airplanes, Clarence being adept at the latter.]

June 15, 1923 (Friday)

Dearest Frank,

The other day when Clarence did not get a card and Francis and I did, he said "sniff, sniff! Papa forgot me," and every day when the mail comes, he wants to know if there is anything from you to him. He cried two nights this week with leg ache...For dinner today we had fried chicken, gravy, fresh peas, stuffed eggs and hot biscuits. The boys seem to enjoy my cooking.

[Josie]

June 17, 1923 (Sunday)

Dearest Josie,

Had my first good sleep since I left home and am fine and dandy this morning. Had the same breakfast we usually have at home. Heard the mockingbirds and roosters early this morning, another reminder of home. Tell Clarence I got some samples of rocks at the Grand Canyon for his geology collection. Tell Francis to read all he can on the Grand Canyon and he will enjoy it all the more. ..

With much love, Frank

June 20, 1923 (Wednesday)

Dearest Josie,

I went through the red tape of registration [at Stanford] yesterday. They have the details all worked out to a fine point. Even had my picture taken on one of the steps…Immense is the best word to describe the University…Your letter was awaiting me. It made me feel just a little homesick and wonder just why I was way out here for.

With love to all, Frank

June 23, 1923 (Saturday)

Dearest Frank,

We got home from Shiner without any trouble. When we drove in, Clarence began to cry …and said, "I don't like to come home without Papa." He has dropped his mouth down several times. That night when he went to bed and the next morning at the breakfast table he said, "I miss Papa and I want to go with you when you go to see him." This surely was a big empty house Wednesday evening…

The boys are just fine and help do the things around the place. Francis does the dishes all the time. I am going for the ice now…Well say good night.

Heaps of love, Your Wifie

[Editor's note: Frank Guittard's former Welhausen in-laws lived in Shiner, Texas where Francis and Clarence frequently visited their cousins, aunts, and uncles.]

June 25, 1923 (Monday)

Dear Papa,

I hope the weather will not be as cold when we get to California as you said it was…The hens laid poorly today and I got only one egg, two others having been broken. It looks like the hen pecked a hole in the end. Have had only two setters so far, discharging one today and catching another. Mama Josie has kept me at work scrubbing the porch, drying the dishes, etc. Lawns seem hard to get…I took our thermometer out in the sun and it registered 110…I will have to stop writing now as Mama Josie wants me to take a bath.

With love, Francis

[Editor's note: Francis, who would later become a successful attorney and trial lawyer, was skilled at advocacy from an early age. In high school he earned extra money mowing neighbors' lawns when he could get the jobs.]

June 27, 1923 (Wednesday)

[Dearest Frank]

Do you smell my new blackberry preserves? I put up six and one half quarts of jam today and went to a "42" party this morning...

[Josie]

[Editor's note: "42" was a popular trick-taking game that supposedly originated in Texas and was played with dominoes before the advent of television, along with dominoes, Monopoly, checkers, canasta, and other games people played around a card table. One advantage of "42" was that although it involved the taking of tricks, unlike Contract bridge, Spades, and Euchre, it was not considered a "card" game and therefore could pass scrutiny by the Southern Baptists who refused to play card games on moral grounds, i.e., that playing card games constituted gambling. "42" was considered Texas' "National Game."]

June 29, 1923 (Friday)

Dearest Josie,

It is certainly nice and kind of you to write so often. Don't expect too much from me. I am a busy man. Wednesday is my busiest day, four hours in the class room. Then each teacher assigns enough work to keep you entirely employed on his course alone. I am taking four courses under as many different teachers...

I am glad to hear a good report from Francis and that Clarence is losing some of his terrors for the water. Well, yes, I get a little homesick sometimes but I have cancelled about twelve days off the calendar and there are not so many more. I hope you are not wearing yourself to a frazzle working on those floors....

With much love, Frank

July 1, 1923 (Sunday)

Dear Mama Josie,

Aunt Henrietta is sure treating me nice. Clarence is getting along all right but he didn't show much respect for me when I went over there last time. I couldn't make him stop because Mrs. Mewes might send an unfavorable report of me home…Elmer came over and played the piano for me the other night. He can sure play jazz but that's all…Clarence was up to eleven o'clock last night at the fair as well as Ray and myself. I will have to close as Sunday school soon takes up.

With Love, Francis

[Editor's notes: Francis was writing from Shiner where he and Clarence were staying with Mamie's cousins. Mrs. Mewes, sometimes called "Auntie Mama," was a family friend in Shiner who helped Eliza Amsler Welhausen (Mamie's mother) take care of Clarence before Frank's marriage to Josie. The fair was probably a local one sponsored by local merchants and farmers. Elmer was a friend of Francis who lived in Shiner.

Frank had encouraged Francis to play the works of classical composers for the piano rather than those of the popular composers (ragtime, jazz, etc.). Again, Francis showed his skills as an advocate.]

July 3, 1923 (Tuesday)

Dear Sweetheart,

I am getting used to the shower bath. Did not like it at first. All bathtubs were taken out some years ago to prevent upper classmen from hazing the freshmen...

With much love, Frank.

[Editor's note: Hazing was also a problem at Baylor during the tenure of long-time Baylor President Rufus C. Burleson, who presided over the school at Independence (1851-1861), and later in Waco (1886-1897). Between those tenures he was president of Waco University which was merged into Baylor at Waco in 1886.

Frank's house at 1401 South 8th Street had only tub baths until sometime in the 1930s. As a teenager, Clarence held out for a shower bath when Frank and Josie were planning house renovations.]

July 3, 1923 (Tuesday)

Dearest Lover,

Have just fed the chicks and Kitty. During the day the kitty follows me wherever I go until I have to put him outside. He is lonesome for someone to play with. I can hardly tie my shoes because he pulls the strings so...

[Josie]

[Editor's note: This kitty was probably the white kitty that Frank was bathing when President Brooks telephoned. According to Josie, Clarence, who answered the telephone, told President Brooks that Frank was giving the cat a bath and could not come to the phone. See the postcard below, dated August 16 in which Frank refers to Clarence's white kitty.]

July 8, 1923 (Sunday)

Dear Sweetheart,

The town of Palo Alto is a mile from the University. The two are connected by a driveway lined on each side by palms and walks...

From my experience I can make a few suggestions that will help you enjoy the trip. Firstly take a box of Vaseline to keep your nose and lips in condition while in New Mexico and Arizona. The air is so dry that it is needed very much. I could have used twice or three times as many handkerchiefs. Those I had looked like I had stanched a wound. Francis especially with his nose inclined to catarrh should use Vaseline. Some oranges will help too...

With much love, Frank

[Editor's note: Frank used the "driveway" daily to walk from the Stanford Campus to Palo Alto and back.]

[Editor's note on President Brooks' battles: On July 9, J. Frank Norris sent President Brooks a letter challenging him to a debate on the question of whether the Bible was both scientifically and historically correct. This letter was one of many letters Norris sent to President Brooks during the 1920s attempting to provoke Brooks either into a live debate or to make statements on the record regarding the teaching of evolution at Baylor. On more than one occasion Norris offered Brooks air time on his radio station.]

July 10, 1923 (Tuesday)

Dearest Sweetheart,

Did your vaccinations give you any trouble? All the checks are gratefully received. Got ten gallons of gas Sunday at 19 cents per...

Lots of love, Your wifie

July 12, 1923 (Thursday)

Dearest Josie,

With regard to the timing of your trip, I can manage the examinations all right. I had one today and the terrors are somewhat subsided. They are not so bad after all…

Lovingly, Frank

July 13, 1923 (Friday)

Dearest Sweetheart,

I made 19 glasses of plum jelly and 5 quarts of plum butter yesterday and today. There seems to be plenty of plums but peaches are selling 30 cents per dozen and of course at that price I will not preserve any. We had a watermelon yesterday and it was a good one to the tune of 40 cents…Well say goodbye—

Lots of love, Your wifie.

July 19, 1923 (Friday)

Dearest Sweetheart,

I have been working pretty hard this week so as not to get behind...

Lovingly, Frank.

P.S. Tell Clarence I have some samples of rocks from the Grand Canyon and also from the mountain near the Joaquin Miller home to add to his collection.

July 19, 1923 (Friday)

Dearest Frank,

Infant Francis left the water running all night last night…

[Josie]

[Editor's note: Francis was evidently responsible for keeping the yard watered during the summer. Running the water all night would have been a needless expense which would have irritated frugal Josie, who was in charge of the household in Frank's absence.]

July 23, 1923 (Monday)

DEAR PAPA,

WE HAVE GOOD TIMES SWIMMING AT THE FISH POND. KISS
(drawing) HUG (drawing)

CLARENCE

[Editor's note: The Fish Pond was a local swimming club in Waco.]

July 23, 1923 (Monday)

Dear Sweetheart,

Say you will have to smile when I tell you your little new rooster is making a peculiar sound that I am sure he thinks [he] is a crow. The one in the chicken yard still fights me. Some days ago I gave him such a lick on the head that he staggered for a little while—I thought maybe we would have to eat rooster that day...

Well say goodnight. Time for little [Sonny] to go to bed.

Lots of love—Your wifie.

[Editor's note: The editor is advised that roosters are eaten just like hens, but the former tend not to have as much meat on them.]

[Editor's note on President Brooks' battles: On July 23, J. Frank Norris sent a letter to President Brooks referring to Brooks' defense of Baylor science professors Lula Pace and O. C. Bradbury against Norris' charge of teaching evolution and Brooks' view on God's creation of the world as a "process." In the letter, Norris invited Brooks to appear with him on the public square in Cleburne, where Norris' topic would be "The Bible vs. Modernism and Evolution." To Norris and other anti-evolutionists, the word "process" was just another word for "evolution."]

July 25, 1923 (Wednesday afternoon)

Dearest Lover,

Do you smell the plum preserves that I am cooking? Francis got almost two of those galvanized iron buckets full from the plum tree on the 7th Street lot...

You will surely be surprised to know Clarence has lost all his fear of the water. Swims, with his wings, face under water, besides other stunts. Surely is proud of himself. ...

Well say goodbye and go stir my plums—

Lots and lots of love, Josie

[Editor's note: The "7th Street lot" may have been one of Frank or Josie's rent house locations.]

July 26, 1923 (Thursday)

Dearest Josie,

Wednesday I finished reading my paper which was discussed in the class longer than any yet presented. The Professor even thanked me for the paper when I finished reading it. My subject was "The Emancipation of the Slaves in Brazil"...

That fruit closet must be looking wonderfully fine. ....Wish I were with you.

With much love, Frank.

July 30, 1923 (Monday)

[Dear Frank],

Clarence slept with me the past two nights and when I went to bed last night, he was not asleep—His latest: "Mama Josie, can cats hatch kittens without a mama and papa?" My answer: "I think not." "Well Mama Josie, can babies be born without a mama & papa""—Again, "I think not". Clarence: "Not with just a Mama?" Said Brother Francis had told him that....

Lovingly, Josie

[Editor's note: It sounds like fifteen-year-old Francis was teasing six-year-old Clarence.]

August 2, 1923 (Thursday)

Dearest Lover,

That little girl died this morning from blood poisoning caused from picking a pimple on her face. Last night after we got home I went over [to the little girl's house] while I thought both of the boys were in bed but seems that Francis was not. He called me for something and when I did not answer he became alarmed, dressed himself and was out in the yard looking for me when he saw me coming. Said he thought maybe someone had kidnapped me and he was getting ready to start out to hunt for me...

Lots of love---Josie

[Editor's note: There is no doubt that a little girl died. The asserted cause, the picking of a pimple, sounds like neighborhood gossip.]

[Editor's note on President Brooks' battles: In August President Brooks made a strong personal attack on J. Frank Norris in defense of Baylor on the radio. In Brooks' archived notes made apparently for this radio address, Brooks referred to Norris as "the leader of the vaudeville performers in the Texas pulpit," claiming that Norris didn't care about evolution at Baylor and that "he would drop Baylor and the theory of evolution and attack the theory of gravitation if by it he could get a bigger crowd to hear him."

Thereafter, Brooks attacked the record of Norris' church of giving to foreign missions and also for only giving $100 after the Carroll Library and Chapel at Baylor burned.]

August 4, 1923 (Saturday)

Dearest Josie,

I have just finished the first draft of another paper. It consisted of a lot of stuff I dug out of the Congressional Record...I have had to dig all this out in horrible detail and present the facts in a fascinating narrative. I spent hours among musty smelling volumes. Thank goodness it is over...It will then be given to another student in the same seminar course and I will get his paper and at the next meeting of the class we will criticize each other's work. Does it not all sound immensely important?...

Lovingly, Frank.

[Editor's note: Frank seems to have felt that he was a little old for this kind of graduate school exercise.]

August 16, 1923 (Thursday)[postcard]

Dear Clarence,

How many cats have you found in Bronte? I know you miss your white kitty. Who is taking care of it? Some of the students here have dogs. Hope you are having a good time.

With love, Papa

[Editor's note: Clarence and Mama Josie were visiting her family in Bronte, Texas. The white kitty to which Frank referred is likely the kitty in the story about the telephone call from President Brooks.]

August 17, 1923 (Friday) [postcard]

Dear Sonnie,

How would you like to see one of those big birds swallow oranges whole?...It looks funny to see the orange go down his throat. We will see Papa Sunday.

Hug, Kiss, Mama Josie.

[Editor's note: The card is addressed to Clarence in Bronte and postmarked Los Angeles.]

September 11, 1923 (Tuesday) [postcard]

Dear Clarence,
We are coming back to Texas as fast as the train can carry us.
Love, Papa

[Editor's note: The postcard is from Pike's Peak.]

June 13, 1924 (Friday)

Dear Papa,

I have been awful busy and I have not had time to write a letter. I am now on the janitor gang and have to get up at 6 [a.]m....to help out on the tennis courts...I was very economical on the train and had a good deal of money left over...

With love, Francis

P.S. Towels, baths, stationery, and soap are furnished free. I take a shower every night.

June 21, 1924 (Saturday)

Dear Mama Josie,

I have changed jobs. I am now a bell hop...I have just gone on duty. Received $1.00 in 48 hours in tips. They are unusually tight as this is a girls' conference. When off duty I either hike, fish or play tennis. I caught my first fish, a rainbow trout, a week ago...I hiked up "Teddy's Teeth" yesterday in an hour and fifty-five minutes, including a ten minutes of rest at the top...I seem to have more stamina and endurance than the other boys...Don't think I have an indoor job. The guests stay in 40 cottages in a circle, each of which holds 8 people...Carry[ing] grips to these is no easy work. Papa wanted me to develop my chest and running up mountains to deliver telegrams and messages sure does it.

Francis

[Editor's note: The rock formations [Teddy's Teeth] on the west side of Rams Horn Mountain were named for, and possibly make fun of, Teddy Roosevelt's teeth.]

June 22, 1924 (Sunday)

Dear Papa,

Went to "Twin Sisters" this morning. It is 1436 feet above sea level…and my first hike above sea level…I was sure petered out at the top, but I nearly ran away from them coming back. They said I did as good or better than any boy in camp. Both have lived in the mountains all their lives…

With love, Francis

[Editor's note: Francis and two college students went on a 20 mile hike up Twin Sisters in the afternoon.]

June 25, 1924 (Wednesday)

Dear Sweetheart,

I wish you were here to help me eat these fine Magee tomatoes. The flowers, the chickens, the cat and Liza are doing finely. Hope Clarence has gotten over his trouble. Tell him that was a fine letter.

With love to both, Frank

July 15, 1924 (Tuesday)

Dear Papa,

[After chronicling recent adventures in Colorado mountain climbing] I had a wisdom tooth coming through just before I went to Long's Peak (about four days). It hurt me awful-long and I got tonsillitis. I went to see the camp nurse and she painted my tooth and tonsils with iodine. It is well now...

Francis

July 20, 1924 (Sunday)

Dear Mama Josie,

Mr. Lute [in charge of camp employees like Frank] had a reception the other night and he actually let the employees dance at his house. Maybe they are going to suspend the rule on dancing. If he lets them dance at his home, why not elsewhere on the grounds? I had to work that night and did not get to go...

Write oftener. Even the one page letter Papa wrote me the other day was appreciated though. I would like to receive longer ones...You and Papa expect me to keep up a correspondence with both of you while you take turns about writing to me and have to write twice as much as either of you. It isn't quite fair...

Love, Francis

[Editor's note: Francis' fairness argument sounds good, but Frank had to correspond with Josie, Francis, and Clarence, as well as others, including his correspondence students at Baylor, officials and colleagues at Baylor, and so on. And, of course, Frank was a full-time Ph.D. student as well.]

July 28, 1924 (Monday)

Dear Mama Josie,

[After reciting specific mountains climbed] Dr. and Mrs. Brooks called today while I was gone. Had hard luck coming down the mountain. Ripped my fingernail plumb off. Will have to see the Doc this afternoon so the camp nurse says. May have to call on you to pay my doctor bill. My fingers were so numb and cold I hardly felt the pain, which was lucky…I have not had any time to read the Bible. Finally decided to read it between hops. Have been doing this for about three or four days and have read through Genesis and Exodus, ninety chapters in all. I will have to hump it to earn that $5.00.

They sure have a keen translation of the New Testament here by Moffat. It reads like a story…My tennis, and especially my serve, is improving. I hope to beat Papa a love set when I get home. My racquet strings are breaking. I will have to have it restrung when I get home. Have to quit and read Leviticus.

Love, Francis

P.S. I would not object to a little more homemade candy if you have time.

August 15, 1924 (Friday)

Dear Papa and Mama Josie,

I received both of your letters. Would prefer if you would not both write at the same time...

[Francis]

August 25, 1924 (Monday)

Dear Papa,

[Regarding a multi-day campout experience] We saw 1 woodchuck, 3 deer, 7 ptarmigan, 5 conies, three big hawks or eagles…and lots of gophers and chipmunks…

I am getting tired of rotten eggs and fruit, moldy bread, condensed milk, no milk to drink, poor service, and hard dry cake. Will be glad to get some good cooking again. Will never kick about the food at home any more. They gave us pancakes big as plates and hard as leather.

Love, Francis

September 7, 1924 (Sunday)

Dear Mama Josie,

The Boy Scout Executive Conference blew in yesterday and I have not had time to write. Between conferences I was put on the boiler gang, sawing, cutting and hauling wood, as well as cleaning out sewer pipes (from the laundry), setting up and carrying stoves, and doing electrical wiring. And now a bell hop again....

Take a shower ice cold every day to stave off colds...

Love, Francis

[Editor's note: Although Frank had his theories about how to avoid colds (see his February 5, 1928 letter infra to Francis), taking ice cold showers in Colorado was probably not among them.]

[Editor's note on President Brooks' battles: In September, J. Frank Norris preached at Fair Park Auditorium in Dallas against the theory of evolution, Baylor University, and President Brooks.

In October, Brooks charged that Norris had offered to pay for spies at Baylor. Norris also sent a telegram to Brooks in October advising that Norris was in the greatest revival campaign of his life at a tabernacle of eight thousand capacity and inviting Brooks to appear and explain why he expelled [Dale S.] Crowley "for exposing evolution and...why you expelled him without giving him a hearing...," but that Brooks will be given "a full fair and courteous hearing."

At the end of October, Charles S. Fothergill, who, according to Crowley, espoused evolution while teaching a history class, resigned and President Brooks reluctantly accepted his resignation.

In the spring of 1925, President Brooks called Guy B. Harrison, Jr. to come in and see him. Harrison had no idea what the purpose of the visit might be, but of course obliged President Brooks. The meeting turned out to be an interview for the vacancy in the History Department created by the resignation of Fothergill. Brooks reportedly told Harrison that Professor Guittard had highly recommended him, but Brooks needed to know "whether you think you can teach History 102 and 103 without getting involved in a row over whether the whale swallowed Jonah or not?" Harrison replied that he thought he could do so and took up his new position at Baylor in June 1925.]

June 16, 1925 (Tuesday)

Dear Papa,

I have not written lately as I have been making preparations to climb
Ypsilon...

I climbed Ypsilon...Never saw so much snow I all my life. We were the
first up and climbed the peak earlier than it has ever been climbed...

With love, Francis

July 10, 1925 (Friday, from Shiner)

Dear Papa,

How is Frisky? I am getting along fine at Aunt Edna's. Taking a bath today. How is Mama Josie? We had some rain this afternoon. The creek was out of its banks and the boys here put on their bathing suits and went down it. I am getting lonesome for you.

With love, your boy, Clarence

[Editor's note: All spelling in this letter and the next belong to eight-year-old Clarence.]

[Editor's note on President Brooks' battles: The Scopes "Monkey" Trial commenced July 10 in Dayton, Tennessee and continued until conclusion on July 21. Substitute teacher John T. Scopes was found guilty of violating a Tennessee law (the Butler Act) against teaching the theory of evolution.

This trial was the most highly publicized event of the fundamentalists' holy war of the 1920s and featured Clarence Darrow for the defense, a criminal attorney of national reputation but no professed religious faith, and, for the prosecution, William Jennings Bryan, a gifted orator and thrice defeated Democratic candidate for U.S. president.

Bryan had been brought into the case for the prosecution by the World Christian Fundamentals Association founded by Reverend William Bell Riley who had received his theological training at Southern Baptist Theological Seminary. The American Civil Liberties Union had offered to pay for the defense of anyone prosecuted under Tennessee's anti-evolution law (the Butler Act.)

At some point in 1925, Texas public school textbooks mentioning evolution theory were banned. See the Epilogue for more on the Scopes Trial and its aftermath.]

July 18, 1925 (Saturday, from Shiner)

Dear Mama Josie,

How is Frisky? Auntie Mama says she is going to have a slumber party next Tuesday. I went to the cemetery this morning. I went to Yoakum day before yesterday and went swimming and I can swim a little now, and that night spent the night at Ray's house and we had lots of fun, and Aunt Henrietta told me to do it again.

[Clarence]

August 4, 1925 (Tuesday)

Dear Papa,

It was indeed a surprise to learn that you had your tonsils removed. I thought you were past that stage. I hope you are feeling better now...I have done more hiking than anyone else in camp. It is making me tough as a nail...My roommate and I are now about the best all-around mountaineers in camp...

With love, Francis

August 19, 1925 (Wednesday)

Dear Folks,

I climbed the East Face of Long's Peak yesterday with my roommate...My roommate and I led the way up. I wasn't a bit nervous or scared, even on an eight-inch ledge with 800 feet below me...We had to pull him [another climber] up with the rope quite a ways. We were tied together on the glacier and all the way to the top...A Swiss guide who has climbed the Matterhorn and quite a few other Swiss peaks said that the East Face of Long's Peak is equal to the Matterhorn. It is certainly the hardest climb in Colorado...

How much shall I feed the chickens? Does the lawn need watering too? Isn't it pretty dry by now? It will seem queer to find strange people at home...

With love, Francis

[Editor's note: By "strange people," Francis must be referring to new renters Frank and Josie had let rooms to.]

August 22, 1925 (Saturday)

Dear Mama Josie,

I was glad to get your letter and to hear that nothing bad had happened to Papa. I was beginning to get worried...It looks as if I have a clear road to the tennis championship of camp. I have only two more matches to play, one of them with Burgess. I have been beating him consistently but I will try my best to keep from getting over-confident.

The girls are not bothering me so much now. At first it was a couple of them, then it narrowed down to the one with the most brains and best looks. I thought I was in pretty deep at first, but I am getting so I can take care of myself all right.

With love, Francis

P.S. The pianos here are awful. I have to force myself to play on them and then I doubt whether it does any good or not.

[Editor's note: There is no record of what the health issue was that concerned Francis. Frank may simply have fainted and alarmed Josie. Frank encouraged Francis to play classical piano pieces.]

September 8, 1925 (Tuesday)

Dear Folks,

I am taking care of the chickens. Miss Engleking [a roomer] has charge of Frisky until Thursday. I took a setter [hen] and inflicted solitary confinement upon her this morning. I picked all the fleas off the cat this morning with the tweezers. There were about 729…The car runs fine. The brakes are not quite tight enough, but they are tightening with use. The Baylor cafeteria is sure a rotten place to eat. Miss Engleking is always cussing them out. Spoilt tough meat and hardly any vegetables except 50 varieties of beans and peas. I am going to mow the lawn now.

With love, Francis

[Editor's note: The Baylor cafeteria for students and faculty was undoubtedly somewhere on, or adjacent to, the Baylor campus and near the Guittard house at 1401 South 8th Street in Waco.]

June 16, 1926 (Wednesday, India, Calif.)

Dear Sweetheart,

It would be impossible I suppose to leave home without forgetting something and so I forgot my room receipt about which I wrote from El Paso. If you didn't get the card you will find it in the 2nd right drawer of my desk. It may beat me to Stanford yet. I had hoped to do that fixing—the mop and the closet door--but time went a "fugeing." The next time I go on a trip think I shall begin to pack up a week before starting.

As I go along I have a vision occasionally of Clarence lying so patiently on his bed and of my sweetheart as she said good-by at the station. This reminds me that I forgot something else. I had intended to put those pictures in my trunk. When Clarence gets out again you can take some kodaks of each other and send them or still better have some new photos made...

Love to my Sweetheart, Frank

June 22, 1926 (Tuesday) [postcard from Palo Alto]

Mrs. F.G. Guittard,

[A]wfully glad to hear from home. Glad Clarence is doing so well. Am going through the ordeal of registration.

Love, Frank

June 22, 1926 (Tuesday)

Dearest Josie,

I have unpacked and am ready to go tomorrow. I certainly have a quiet room. It is a corner room with four windows on the 2nd floor under one of the towers of the building. The room is furnished but I will be the sole occupant.... I finished registration and have three courses and of course do not know the nature of the work yet...I congratulate you on your oil check. May they continue to increase in amount...[My mail box] has no key but a combination lock which I had to fool with some time before I could work it...

Lovingly, Frank.

June 24, 1926 (Thursday)

Dearest Josie,

I am in the midst of it again, and, going finely. I wish you would send me by Parcel Post Hulme's *History of the British People...*, Beasley Forbes Birkett: *Russia from the Vengarians to the Bolsheviks.* I think you will find it in the History office at the University. If you don't find it send Platonof or Platonov-Russia, but I would rather have Beasley etc.'s book. Have been meeting a few of my old student friends, among them Smith from Idaho, the Mormon. Have a dandy room, no flies, no roommate.

Love, Frank

[Editor's note: Frank likely was living in a dormitory this summer.]

June 26, 1926 (Saturday)

Dear Sweetheart,

I went shopping today, visited Woolworth's and purchased a drinking glass, also deposited a correspondence check in the bank. Took dinner at the Russell Cafeteria and of course had some baked salmon and red raspberries...

Lovingly, Frank

June 27, 1926 (Sunday)

Dear Mama Josie,

I tried to dance Friday nite and I'm afraid I made a miserable failure of it. Of course the girl said I was a good dancer, but she couldn't say otherwise…Burgess sure has an easy job. All he seems to do is to eat stuff in the grocery store and sit on the front porch talking to the girls. I have the out-dooringest and one of the hardest jobs in camp and I am sure glad of it…I sure will be glad when the girls leave who are always coming down to play in boots and high heeled shoes. I am getting tired of telling them to vacate…

With love, Francis

June 29, 1926 (Tuesday)

Dear Clarence,

I received your letter with "the Bat" today. No wonder the show was scary if it had something that looked like that picture.

I am glad you liked the folders. It was interesting to see those little alligators eat their dinner. The man threw a piece of meat to them, then each one would grab hold of it, but instead of pulling, they would whirl their bodies around until they twisted a piece off...

The guide [in Yosemite Park] told us there were two hundred bears in the park. The night I stayed at Glacier Point, after we watched the "Fire Falls," a number of us went to the garbage dump to see the bears come to get their supper. When we got there we found one good sized fellow all alone. Having a good time. It wasn't long before a big mother bear and two cubs came out of the brush and up to the dump. She seemed to be pretty savage and made a dash at the first bear which in his hurry to get out of the way ran straight up the hill through the crowd watching them. It was fun to hear the ladies shriek and run, even some of the men gave the bear plenty of room to get back to the woods. Of course, I patted him on the back as he passed me...

I am glad you are well enough to do some planting, I am sure with all that rain, the morning glories...[and the] sunflowers.

With love, Papa

[Editor's note: The show Frank must be writing about which Clarence had seen was a 1926 silent film entitled The Bat featuring an old mansion and a caped killer (the "Bat") who was systematically killing off visitors to the mansion.]

July 3, 1926 (Saturday)

Dearest Sweetheart,

I have just come back from Palo Alto. Smith and I have a course under that Austrian professor Pribraus and we have a meeting once a week to go over our notes together. It was a little difficult to follow him at first but it's gradually going better and we are getting deep into the secret negotiations of European chancelleries…

I get a little hungry for home news. These papers out here are of course full of local and state news. For the first week they were full of large headlines and entire columns and even pages about "Aimee," "Aimee," "Aimee." It looks very much as though Aimee McPherson concocted a scheme to enable her to get some advertising. I suppose you have read about her supposed kidnapping…

I am certainly glad to know that Dr. Harrington [next door neighbor on South 8th Street] takes such a friendly interest in Clarence. The picture shows his arms looking pretty skinny and it will take some time for him to get back to normal…

[Frank]

[Editor's note: Aimee Semple McPherson, Los Angeles Pentecostal, fundamentalist evangelist, revivalist, and faith-healer in the 1920s and 1930s, was supposedly kidnapped. However, later news reports suggested it was a hoax of some kind, perhaps to garner publicity for the church she founded, The International Church of the Foursquare Gospel.]

July 8, 1926 (Thursday)

Dearest Josie,

We had a norther yesterday but today was the usual weather a little warm at noon but cool morning and evening. I have used that third blanket nearly every night. My overcoat came in handy several times on my trip and some nights I wore it in my room while studying to keep from getting chilled...

Give my love to the folks

With love, Frank

July 11, 1926 (Sunday)

Dear Sweetheart,

Sunday is a long day. Went to the beautiful church this morning and heard a good sermon by Dean Brown of Yale University... You have been very sweet to write so often. Don't wait for me to write as there isn't much to happen here--it's all work.

I do get a few snacks occasionally. I was downtown-- paid 15 cents for a shine and 65 cents for a haircut (at home it is 10 & 50)...then stepped over to a market to get some fruit. I picked out a dozen nice ripe yellow apricots about the size of ordinary peaches. Imagine my surprise when the man told me I owed him the sum of five cents. I fell over backwards but recovered sufficiently to produce a nickel.

I am paying double the price I did before for the privilege of having a room to myself but it is worth it...

Lovingly, Frank

[Editor's note on President Brooks' battles: On July 17, J. Frank Norris shot and killed unarmed Dexter Chipps in Norris' office at the First Baptist Church in Fort Worth. Chipps, who was not a member of Norris' church, was a supporter of Fort Worth's mayor, H.C. Meachum, a political enemy of Norris'. Norris was later tried for Chipps' murder but pleaded self-defense; after a highly publicized trial, the jury found him not guilty.]

July 18, 1926 (Sunday)

Dear Sweetheart,

Yes, four weeks are gone and I am not sorry. The days are so full that the weeks fly pretty rapidly. The only way I can keep off what might be called homesickness is to be doing something...Did sonny boy get to sleep in "an upper?" ..I believe I prefer them. ...I don't bump my head when I dress. Then one is farther away from the big fat snorers who usually have to take the lowers...

I have had my shower bath and am ready for breakfast which comes at 8 o'clock on Sun. morning at the Union. I think it gets daylight here sooner than at the same time at home so I never can sleep very late and have plenty of time mornings. I have one 8 o'clock recitation...

Lovingly F.G. Guittard

[Editor's note: A reference to snoring pops up occasionally in Frank's letters and is possibly connected to his obsession with avoiding colds. No doubt he would have sympathized with Texas outlaw Sam Bass' antipathy for snorers, which is recorded in a famous story about Bass called "Death by Snoring."]

July 23, 1926 (Friday 10 p.m.)

Dearest Josie,

I am just in from the library where I have [been] cramming for a test for next week. All my professors this time believe in tests. Last week I had two and this week one. On these I made two A's and one B.

As to my eyes they have been doing finely. The one with the bum tear duct does not bother me unless I get in the cool wind. Those "drops" all escaped from the dropper during my trip—the rubber cap was removed in some way…

Hooray! Five weeks are gone!

Lovingly, Frank

July 24, 1926 (Saturday)

Dear Papa,

I have been doing my work very successfully, and also playing tennis successfully. Burgess and I have played six sets so far and I got five. The one he got was 6-4 and the last one I got was 6-1…

I saw in the Denver Post where Norris killed a man. I suppose that will about put the quietus on his activities…

With Love, Francis

[Editor's note on President Brooks' battles: The murder trial of J. Frank Norris did not put the "quietus on his activities." However, his reputation was not improved by the sensational trial; the prosecution and defense agreed that Norris had shot and killed Dexter Chipps who was unarmed.]

August 1, 1926 (Sunday)

Dear Clarence,

That was a nice long letter—yes, it was a surprise to me. You write better than brother Francis. I did not realize that your penmanship was so good, you must have been practicing since school closed. It is a good accomplishment to be a good penman. I think if you keep on you will be an expert. Just follow Mama Josie's directions and I know you will.

About Frisky, it seems to me he ought to be using that fourth foot by this time. Probably you should take him to the veterinarian…One of the boys in the dormitory here has a cat. He gets some milk every morning and divides up with his pet…One boy caught a snake and kept it in a box in his room for several days but he got orders to take it out…

Lovingly, Papa

[Editor's note: Frank's handwriting in his letters to his family shows his own handwriting was practiced and skillful. He likely developed this skill during his course under W. W. Franklin at Baylor, the Giant Rhetoric Class, which stressed, among other things, good penmanship.]

August 7, 1926 (Saturday)

Dear [Francis],

Well, there is not much news here, it is all work, work. I made 96 on a test last week but my grades are not all like that. Three weeks more and then a vacation. I think I should like to get off somewhere so I could not see a book.

Lovingly, Papa

[Editor's note: It is hard to imagine Frank without a book in his hands, but perhaps a golf club would have sufficed for a few hours.]

August 13, 1926 (Friday)

Dear Francis,

I sent you some popular music the first of the week and something else today. Hope you received both ok. There is a good music store in Palo Alto and if you give me the names of some pieces you would like to have, I will send them. Just now I am terribly busy on a paper. I will not be able to really enjoy life until I have it off my hands. In about two weeks I shall be speeding toward Texas.

Lovingly, Papa

August 28, 1926 (Saturday)

Dearest Josie and Clarence,

I just got your letter and "hello." My last exam came this morning from 10 to 12. I got up this morning at 4:30 to cram but am feeling fine because it is all over.

Lovingly, Frank

August 31, 1926 (Tuesday)

Dear Francis,

I have gone the limit on sightseeing and tourist matters for this year. Then I have very little time left for doing a good deal of work before the opening of the fall quarter [at Baylor]. I feel like taking it a little easy for a while as I have had a strenuous summer's work. Like a dunce I signed up for four courses and I was pursued all summer, but I think I came out pretty well. I had four exams the last three days of last week, Thursday, Friday, and Saturday…

Well I am glad to know that you are taking some pride in your individual initiative. I hope it will extend and take in some of the little things that go to make home an agreeable place. It is of course an old truism that little things go to make up life. These cannot be neglected without making life a real tragedy. A thoughtless word, an act of neglect to those who are interested in you and love you, leaves a wound that does not heal for days.

Being away from home for the past three months has given me an opportunity to think over many things in relation to our home life. There is room for improvement for all of us. So when I say that I hope your initiative will extend to doing your part in keeping home orderly in the house as well as around the place, to helping to create a brighter and happier atmosphere in the home, I do not mean to say that the others cannot do more.

Then while I have a little leisure, I should like to suggest something else for you to think over. I am writing from my own experiences in life. No one advised me or suggested what I should study for or take up as a life work. As a result when my judgment was immature as it is with everyone before coming in contact with the practical affairs of life, I can look back now and see that I made some very serious mistakes. It is folly and a waste of time and life to make mistakes that might be avoided by profiting by the experiences of others. So immaturity of judgment can be corrected by consulting with those who have had a varied experience in life. There are many sides to every question. Learn to profit by the experiences of others.

If the race did not know its past history, progress would be very slow as we often hear but this is still more true of the individual. I would regret for you to blunder along as I have done and be driven by circumstances instead of mapping out a line of action and working to it. That is make everything contribute directly or indirectly to some definite object. Well I could write much more but probably I have written enough or too much.

I hope you liked those last pieces of music I sent.

Lovingly, Papa

[Editor's note: This letter of Frank's, while mostly vague as to specific courses of action for Francis to follow insofar as what to study and what to take up as a vocation, is nevertheless, very clear that Frank thought he made big mistakes himself, and wanted to help Francis avoid making the same ones. The editor will treat this theme at length in The Life & Times, the goal being to identify from the evidence what Frank possibly thought his mistakes had been and what course of action in 1926 he possibly felt he should have pursued in 1886 and years following.

Of course, Frank in 1926 did not have the opportunity to see his life from the vantage point of his last few years or how his life would be perceived today by those who came after, including his students. He possibly would have modified his views later as he grew older and became more forgiving of his early choices and decisions.]

September 1, 1926 (Wednesday, Hotel Utah)

Dear Sweetheart,

As far as I can figure out, I get in Waco Sat[urday] at 12 or 1 o'clock at night. I will not expect you to meet me at that unearthly hour. Salt Lake City is as fine as ever.

Lovingly, Frank

I may beat this letter to Waco.

September 3, 1926 (Friday) [postcard from Salt Lake]

[To Clarence]
If you were here, we would go for a swim in Salt Lake.
Papa

[Editor's note on President Brooks' battles: In November, Dale Crowley's attorney sent Baylor a letter asserting Crowley's right to a hearing on his suspension from the university.]

June 18, 1927 (Saturday)

Dear Mamma Josie,

Thank you for the chewing gum. Everyone in our cabin enjoyed it....I swam fifty yards yesterday and am going to do it again today...With love, Clarence. P.S. Please bring me my 3 ply water wheel, my little pillow (for pillow fights) and something to eat.

Clarence [from camp]

[Editor's note: The year of this card cannot be determined, but the content suggests 1927.]

June 25, 1927 (Saturday)

Dear Papa,

My position here [Moraine Lodge, Estes Park, Colo.] is "cook's helper." I have to get up at 4:30 in the morning to start the fires...I am more able to take care of myself than Mama Josie thinks. This position is the highest paid of any here, except those of laundry, foreman, chef, pastry cook, and head waitress. No one under thirty years of age gets a larger wage than I do. That's not bad, is it?

With love, Francis

P.S. This is not my pen, so you may not be able to read it.

June 29, 1927 10 p.m. (Wednesday)

Dearest Josie,

Am just in from the Library. I see I have three letters from you and to have a clear conscience and peaceful slumber, I will answer them at once. I am glad you deposited that check. The first lesson came in before the card but I thought it would come after.

The photos are splendid. You know I have given them a prominent place in my room. Clarence's pictures are good too, but I believe I like his expression better in the individual picture than in the one with you.

The extension came today and I will read myself to sleep as usual tonight...

Lovingly, Frank

[Editor's note: By "extension" Frank probably meant his correspondence course papers.]

July 3, 1927 (Sunday)

Dear Sweetheart,

I attended church as usual this morning and was invited in the pew with President Jordan. It happened thusly: a former Baylor student and myself ...came to the entrance of the church just as President Jordan and his wife or secretary—entered. We followed them down the aisle and when the old gentleman stopped to lift the cord at the entrance of the pew, he looked around and seeing us said, "Come in here—there is plenty of room and the people will think I have a lot of guests," so we filed in and took our seats very sanctimoniously...

Lovingly, Frank

[Editor's note: Stanford Emeritus President, David Starr Jordan, a distinguished scholar, ichthyologist, and eugenicist, and Jane Stanford, wife of Leland Stanford, were largely responsible for building Stanford University in its early years with the monies provided by Leland and Jane Stanford. Jordan and Mrs. Stanford, however, did not always see eye-to-eye on how to spend the Stanfords' money. After her death allegedly from strychnine poisoning, it was speculated that he may have covered-up the cause of death to protect the reputation of the young university.

Jordan also authored a charming illustrated volume of children's nonsense stories, The Book of Knight and Barbara (1899), which was read to Clarence as a child and likely purchased while Frank was in residence in Palo Alto.]

July 6, 1927 (Wednesday night)

Dear Sweetheart,

Glad to get Clarence's letter [even] if it was second hand. I suppose he did not have much time for letter writing. I hope he will not do much bathing in the old creek swimming hole. I am afraid that is what caused Glade's (a cousin of Clarence's) fever. The only realization I had of a holiday was the procession of cars along the highway as I went to supper. I am settling down to a monotonous routine but like my work.

Lovingly, Frank

July 9, 1927 (Saturday night)

Dear Sweetheart,

You certainly are becoming ambitious to mow the lawn. Will you let me sit in the swing when I come home while you urge the lawnmower?

Lovingly, Frank

[Editor's note: Lawns in those days were mowed with push mowers, not gas- or electric-powered mowers.]

July 13, 1927 (Wednesday)

Dear Sweetheart,

I felt real guilty when I found out from your letter that the pictures were for [our] anniversary because I realized for the first time that I had not thought of our June 10th anniversary in the arrangements for leaving, etc. but I shall try to make up for it. You should have reminded the "absent minded professor" in some way.

Lovingly, Frank

July 14, 1927 (Thursday)

[Dearest Frank],

Judge West was buried yesterday.... He looked as though he was only asleep. Wore his Confederate gray suit and had his Confederate pin on the lapel of his coat. Also had the Confederate flag on his casket...

Lots of love and hug and kiss—Josie

[Editor's note: Judge John C. (Camden) West became principal of Waco Trinity River and Classical School and later president of Waco University before its merger in 1886 with Baylor University at Independence. In 1861, he enlisted in Speight's Regiment of the Confederate Army, and Rufus C. Burleson succeeded him as president of Waco University. He published his diary and war letters in A Texan in Search of a Fight *(1901). A portion of Baylor's current campus originally belonged to Judge West and another portion belonged to Colonel Joseph Warren Speight.*

We suspect that Frank and Josie had different views of the Civil War, Frank siding with the Union and Josie siding with the Confederacy, and that the topic was avoided at 1401 South 8th Street.]

July 17, 1927 (Sunday morning before breakfast)

Dear Sweetheart,

You are awful nice and good and sweet to write so often. Then in one letter you remind me that you love me. Well it is a good plan to actually say it sometimes but you remind me of it in many ways…

Tell Clarence to give me a full account of one time while at Shiner when he went in the creek swimming with the others and not leave anything out…

I wish I had some of that good jelly out here. I am glad to know that the new grapes are doing something. I think I shall gradually plant other vines around the arbor and eliminate the old vine. I visited my neighbor [in the boarding house] and found that he had just hung up his week's laundry on the line in his room. When I saw my last two weeks' laundry bill, I almost decided something of the same kind was necessary, it was $3.12…

[Frank]

July 20, 1927 (Wednesday night)

Dear Sweetheart,

Glad to know you are maintaining amicable relations as well as laundry connections with Maggie. Probably we can avoid the usual dearth of help in the fall.

Lovingly, Frank

July 21, 1927 (Thursday)

Dear Papa,

I have only a short time off. Consequently I have not been able to put much work in [on] shorthand. It takes about an hour to get started studying the stuff…I get snatches of time in which to read, though. I have read a good deal in the German Testament at night before going to bed. I have to dress up to go somewhere to write like I am doing now. There is no table in the bunkhouse.

If it is not too much trouble for you, I wish you would send me a cheap copy of Blackstone's Commentaries. I will send you the money almost immediately on Aug 1….I can read the Commentaries in odd moments. It is almost impossible for me to study shorthand here. I will have to defer it until I get home.

I have been eating Fleischmann's Yeast once a day. My complexion is entirely cleared up and I am not such a bad looking guy. I have gained about 12 pounds, so that I now weigh about 162. The first week I was here at Moraine Lodge I couldn't do a decent "job" to save my neck. After that I began acquiring a few regular habits and drinking lots of water. I now have no trouble at all.

With love, Francis

(Francis from YMCA Camp, Estes Park, Colorado)

[Editor's note: Around this time, Fleischmann's Yeast was touted as being a cure for acne if three cakes were consumed daily.]

August 12, 1927 (Friday)

Dear Mama Josie,

I got a card from Dixie Lynn at Cairo, Egypt not long ago…

With love, Francis

P.S. don't worry about me getting married, as you seemed to say in one of your letters. I have no such intentions, either now or later.

[Editor's note: Francis eventually married Dixie Lynn Wood six years later and had two children with her, Stephen Wood Guittard and Philip Alwin Guittard. Josie and Frank wanted Francis to get a law degree and then a law job before getting married.]

August 15, 1927 9 p.m. (Monday)

Dear Sweetie,

I got all the books you wanted except one, at the Baylor Library. I will pay the public library for that one. I looked through the list of Roosevelt books and there are 36 in all...

I feel like you are making splendid progress—I am real proud of you. All things good or bad always come to an end. Sonny and I went to a show this evening and we are just about ready to go to bed...

Lots of love, Josie

[Editor's note: Frank's dissertation topic was "Roosevelt and Conservation." The Roosevelt was environmentalist and U.S. President Theodore Roosevelt.]

September 2, 1927 (Friday)

Dear Mama Josie and Papa,

As yet I am not sure just when I will get home...I want to play some tennis after I get home. I haven't been beat all summer and so I naturally won't improve much, playing those whom I can beat...

[For next summer]...I was told...that I would have no trouble in getting a license [as a park guide]. That would be the kind of a job I would like. It would certainly give me a good physique without being too strenuous for I would have to go much slower when with parties...I have learned [this summer]...especially about people. Mrs. McPherson wants me to be combination guide and host, next summer, so I must not be entirely lacking in a few of the social graces. She wants me to arrange parties, musical events, features, sing-songs, stunts, athletic events, etc...

Just keep my bed made from Sept 12 to 20...

With love, Francis

[Editor's note: Mrs. McPherson's exact role at the Y.M.C.A. camp is not clear, but she was apparently a person in authority at the camp and not the controversial faith healer.]

[Editor's note on President Brooks' battles: In September, President Brooks wrote The Baptist Standard published by the Baptist General Convention of Texas, to push back against its editorial policy. The Baptist Standard, Brooks felt, had a practice of occasionally publishing unfounded charges against Baylor without giving Brooks a chance during pre-publication to provide Baylor's point of view.

President Brooks also wrote to Reverend William Bell Riley, the organizer of the World Christian Fundamentals Association, and politely, but firmly, asked Riley to refrain from suggesting that Baylor University was in any way associated with the WCFA.

On November 22, the Southern Baptist Convention Radio broadcast an attack on J. Frank Norris and his actions in support of his anti-evolution views.

The program featured President Brooks and others on the same side of the issue. Norris later referred to this broadcast as a "hate-fest." Brooks' mail after the broadcast was mixed, and there was a difference of opinion among his supporters as to whether he had helped Baylor against Norris' attacks.

Brooks himself had, from the beginning of the controversy, attempted to avoid making the controversy personal between him and Norris, but finally gave in to the pressure to speak his mind over the radio. Norris' apparent animus against Brooks suggested the controversy was always partly personal for Norris.

In December, Norris challenged Lee R. Scarborough, president of Southwestern Baptist Theological Seminary, to speak on the topic of the conspiracy Norris claimed was mounted against him. Norris also asserted, without proof, that Fort Worth Mayor H.C. Meacham sent Dexter Chipps to assassinate him in July 1926.]

January 2, 1928 (Monday) [Los Angeles; on the Sunset Limited]

Dear Sweetheart,

We arrived here on the minute. Had a good trip. California always looks good after crossing the desert. I am taking advantage of the writing desk in the observation car while they are switching us around some here in Los Angeles...

The orange groves look beautiful where the ripe fruit is still hanging. There seems to have been much rain and the landscapes do not have the brown and bare appearance they do in summer time. After a night's ride I shall be at my destination...

With love, Frank

January 3, [1928] (Tuesday)

Dear Sweetheart,

I am settled at the above address [527 Waverly St., Palo Alto, Calif.]. I scouted around a little before going out to the campus to see what I could find in the way of a room. The rooms on the campus I found were all higher priced than this one and not more desirable so I came back here. I pay $18.00 per month. My room is on the second floor and faces the Episcopal Pastor's home who lives by himself. There are no children in this house, only the man and his wife so I think I shall have a quiet place…

I registered this morning, got my registration book in which the courses are signed up but did not sign up for any work as Dr. Robinson will not be in until this afternoon. I walked back to town for lunch and to get my room in order. It is a grey day but the ground is all green under the trees on the campus and over the hills…

I am feeling fine today and ready for work. Hope all are well at home.

Lovingly, Frank

[Editor's note on President Brooks' battles: Since Frank was in Palo Alto, he would not have been in Waco to hear of certain remarks made by President Brooks in Baylor chapel on this day [January 3, 1928]. President Brooks addressed rumors circulating since sometime in December 1927 that certain Baptists were strongly considering the removal of Baylor University to Dallas, Texas. These rumors, reported in the Baylor Lariat on January 4, 1928 and which ultimately turned out to be true, would have been worrisome to Frank who was sixty-one and had lived in Waco since 1902, residing at 1401 South 8th Street with Josie since 1920. President Brooks stated in chapel that he took no position on the removal proposal, although he did not expect Baylor to move to Dallas. The Baylor community was also informed in the same issue of the Lariat that the Convention had appointed a committee of eighteen to consider the relocation proposal.

The rumors would also have been upsetting to Josie who had many friends in Waco and was active in several local organizations. Josie would have mailed Frank the January 4th issue almost immediately. Of course, Frank was already deep into his Ph.D. work at Stanford, having commenced his late-life pursuit of a Ph.D. in 1923. He must have thought, or at least hoped, that Brooks' strong suggestion that department chairs obtain their Ph.D.'s would constitute the last big interruption he and Josie would have to contend with in their senior years, yet here was President Brooks apparently saying that a credible movement was afoot to relocate Baylor, its faculty, and student body to Dallas. Frank will comment on the movement to relocate Baylor in several letters hereafter.]

January 5, 1928 (Thursday)

Dear Sweetheart,

I walk out to the University every morning and eat breakfast at the Union and get my mail, then spend most of the morning at work in the Library. To clear out the cobwebs of my brain, I then walk to town for lunch and to my room for a rest. I ride back after dinner for library work or a seminar. At 5:30 Belk and I hit the asphalt for town. In that way I walk over four miles a day. I may later cut out the car ride when my walking machine gets to performing smoothly. So far I have arranged some work in my rooms each night.

I have an agreeable room with the one drawback that I have a heater for wood and coal rather than a gas stove...It goes somewhat against the grain to have to haul up coal & kindling and build fires. Fortunately the Heatrola is in the room under me and I do not need much fire and only at night...At noon I use my morning paper for heating purposes or my Literary Digest and get along finely for the short time I am in my room...The landlady has dedicated an aluminum teakettle to my use for heating my water for tonsorial purposes in the morning down in the kitchen. While it is heating I take my exercises without disturbing the pots and pans or apples and potatoes which look at me wonderingly from various nooks and corners.

There is a hot water heater down in the kitchen which connects with the bathtub upstairs and I have received minute instructions as to its proper use and find that it works finely but the landlady is not very enthusiastic about my utilizing it too often, I suppose it has some encouraging effect on the gas bill. But fortunately I am not over enthusiastic about bathing facilities myself...

Lovingly, Frank

[Editor's note: The Heatrola was a coal-burning, warm-air stove manufactured by the Estate Stove Company. Not all consumers were enthusiastic about coal-burning stoves, as they emitted large amounts of black dust.]

January 8, 1928 (Sunday)

Dear Sweetheart,

It helps a whole lot [that you write so often]. Sunday is the hardest day of the week to be away from home. I began today by a walk out University Ave...I stopped at the Snow White Creamery for breakfast and tried those waffles. I think I shall make that a regular part of my Sunday program...

I had leather heels put on my shoes for I did not feel safe on the wet walks these drizzly days.

Lovingly, Frank

[Editor's note: The Snow White Creamery exists in Palo Alto today under a slightly different name and still serves waffles.]

January 11, 1928 (Wednesday)

Dearest Josie,

I have classes only Wed. and Thurs. but I am busy all the time. As to my room, it is fairly comfortable. I get tired regulating my stove. I surely will know how to appreciate good gas when I get home.

You may add to my university address for my correspondence students "Box 584." As I eat breakfast at the Union I have plenty opportunity to get my mail out there. This is the last of the Woolworth tablet...

Lovingly, Frank

January 16, 1928 (Monday)

Dear Sweetheart,

My cold was pretty well gone by the time I got here. I am afraid you caught yours from me. This morning I was real cold. I skated some on a cake of shallow ice not far from the Memorial Church in that quadrangle...

[Frank]

[Editor's note: Frank skated near Mrs. Stanford's re-built Memorial Church on the Stanford Campus.]

January 17, 1928 (Tuesday)

Dearest Josie,

I am in the throes of the process of selecting a thesis subject but don't say anything to nobody...I wish you would send me by air mail or balloon my latest list of theme subjects for History 217 to be found in a drawer on the left of my desk...If any of my friends should make inquiries about my work, be sure to expatiate about this fine California weather, frost, and sunshine these days.

Lovingly, Frank

January 22, 1928 (Sunday)

Dearest Josie,

Your special [delivery] did not reach me before breakfast at the "Snow White Creamery" but soon afterward. I had returned to my room as it was raining and was reading the "Examiner" when the "Special" came.

As to the National Convention, you know San Francisco was also striving to get the convention...Al Smith seems to be running well. How could the hosts refuse their guests from the north to fall in line for Smith? Senator Heflin from Alabama by his injudicious speech has done much to help the Smith cause in the South.

I am going to move the 3rd of February. I have paid for a month here and as soon as it is up, "we vamanose." ...The landlady here has been as nice as could be and doubtless it will shock her terribly to see the transfer man instead of her check the morning of the 3rd... [As to staying in a dormitory] there are many features of dormitory life that do not appeal to me for example radios, phonographs, banjos and vocalizing at all hours of the day and night. I think [the] new place will be more satisfactory. You can't tell though until you try it out. Very innocent looking places I find may develop some alarming nuisances...

For the income tax if there is not sufficient balance I wish you would pay that out of your own fund and I will even up later. I will send you your usual monthly allowance each month and a check for the children's tuition after the March 1st check comes in. By this arrangement we can get along all right for the next two months [and] then there will be easier going. If those three...bills come in, just forward them to me. [Regarding the three overdue merchants' bills]...after all these years of faithful meeting of my obligations, it does not hurt my conscience in the least to make them wait awhile [so we can pay the children's tuition]...

While writing a shower has come up and passed. From my window I am looking down on an orange tree with a number of oranges…They may not be good but I am going to try some of them.

With love to all, Frank

[Editor's note: Frank's reference to Alabama Senator Thomas Heflin's "injudicious speech" was a reference to a vicious speech which the Democrat made in the U.S. Senate four days previously. Heflin attacked the Democratic candidate Al Smith as a Catholic who wanted to put Roman Catholic government above everything and crush Protestantism in America.

Heflin also attacked the Democratic Party for insisting on denouncing the Ku Klux Klan at its convention, Heflin defending the Klan as a Protestant order. Heflin was well known for his inflammatory, demagogic rhetoric as a U.S. Senator. Apparently, Frank, a life-long Democrat, felt, or perhaps hoped, that such an intemperate speech would in fact help Smith, rather than hurt him in the contest against Republican candidate Herbert Hoover. Nevertheless, Hoover was elected.]

January 25, 1928 9:30 am. (Wednesday)

Dear Clarence,

I have had my walk, my waffle, read the paper and next thing is to write a few letters. I feel all puffed up because last week I receive a letter from every member of my family...

[In connection with Belk's recent episode of renal colic] I recognized the symptoms from my own experience. [It was not a case of too much "booze" as passing students surmised.] This morning he seemed to be all right again and talked about getting up. It was an awful experience to go through as I know from two occasions.

Sam [Clarence's dog] is like a bad penny that always comes back or gets back somehow but I suppose you think that is not a very good comparison.

I like to get your letters. Suppose...you write me a full account of what happened at school one day, the most interesting day of the week. Begin with picking up your lunch in the morning and what happened on the way to school, whom you saw and what they said, what you saw along the way, what kind of morning it was. Then about school: tell me about your studying, the recitations, what they were about; what the teacher said, what some of the students said, who "pulled off boneheads," etc. I would like to have a complete history of one day. Of course the play time should be included. What did you do at the different play periods? Write to me as though I were up on the moon and did not know anything about how things went on down on Mother Earth.

Lovingly, Papa

[Editor's note: Norvell C. Belk earned an A.B. from Baylor in 1920 and was an instructor in Baylor's history department. He answered to Frank and was, in all likelihood, one of his former students. Belk was also working on a history degree at Stanford, apparently a master's. As to student "boneheads," Frank collected them in his "Funny Book," particularly the wacky or mullet-headed ones recorded on history exams in his classes.]

January 26, 1928 (Thursday)

Dearest Josie,

From what you report the faculty [Baylor] are keeping up the reputation for babies...Glad to know that Dr. Dawson stays with the First Church [First Baptist Church in Waco]. It would be difficult to get a pastor who could in all respects fill the place better...

Well I finished a piece of investigation work for Dr. Robinson and made my report to him. The task was to find out what had been written in current periodicals on the West or its history from 1920 to January 1928, believe me it was some job...[Dr. Robinson] in commenting on the report said it would be very helpful to him and that it showed that the Stanford Library needed several periodicals which were frequently mentioned...and further that they would be ordered as a result of my report. Stanford has a splendid list of periodicals I found but in the period covered [is missing some that it needs].

Glad to know the hens are paying somewhat for their feed. Weather is fine here. An overcoat is needed here mornings and evenings, but during the middle of the day, may be left at home. I wear mine out in the morning [and] leave it hanging in the library till evening.

Lovingly, Frank

[Editor's note on President Brooks' battles: At the end of January 1928, J. Frank Norris mailed President Brooks a letter Norris claimed he received from a fellow citizen of Brooks in Waco. The letter contained an off-the-wall personal attack against Brooks, which Norris avowed he intended to publish in The Fundamentalist. The author of the letter questioned whether Brooks had ever contributed anything to his community, whether he had ever written a book or pamphlet, or ever taught anyone anything or made any kind of mark as a teacher.

The author of the letter further remarked that Brooks had nothing to show for his twenty-five years leading Baylor and that, where rebuilding the Carroll Chapel and Library was concerned, he should have been able, given his twenty-

five years of experience leading Baylor, to immediately rebuild without mounting a fund raising campaign.]

February 1, 1928 (Wednesday)

Dear Sweetheart,

I sent you the Stanford Daily which gives the infantile paralysis situation here. It is the same as meningitis, I think.....

I still get my breakfast at the "Union," pass the station nearly every morning at 7:30 when the Sunset Limited goes glimmering by. I eat at least one meal at the Mandarin each day then I vary the other one to keep from knowing what I am going to eat before I get there. I find that I eat more fruit since I do not have to carry it so far and I prefer it to the desserts in the eating places. Glad to hear the good reports of the boys.

Lovingly, Frank

[Editor's note: Infantile paralysis (polio) and meningitis can be related but are not the same. A small proportion of people with the poliovirus develop serious complications like paralysis or meningitis. Meningitis is an infection of the covering of the spinal cord and/or brain; however, meningitis can develop from other causes as well including the mycobacterium tuberculosis.

During the 1920s, the Sunset Limited was a passenger train that traveled between New Orleans and Los Angeles on tracks owned by the Southern Pacific Railroad. Currently it is operated by Amtrak. The modern average journey time is approximately 45 hours.]

February 5, 1928 (Sunday)

Dear Francis,

I regret to hear that you still have those ugly colds…Health, efficiency and happiness are very clearly related… in fact…inseparable….You should not be satisfied with temporary palliatives but only with a permanent cure. It is the height of un-wisdom to work hard and prepare for a career if you do not base it upon a permanent foundation of good health. Sooner or later when you are past the blooming vigor of youth and resistance is less strong, disaster will come. Your condition is an abnormal one, the result of perhaps a physical defect of the nasal passages or of a lack of personal care or perhaps both. However, both of these can be remedied.

Once more, are you sufficiently careful: 1) undressing at night, 2) dressing in the morning, 3) taking your bath, 4) changing from one style of clothing to another or from wool to cotton, 5) does tennis bring on your cold? If so, make a careful study to determine what probably caused your cold…It was my purpose that you should follow that consultation we had with Dr. Witte. Do not think that you are saving time or expense or trouble by delaying. There are several personal sacrifices you will have to make at present to avoid greater ones for the future. Evidently you should be more careful about dressing than most boys and not dress as they do if you find it causes trouble. Then it will be necessary to suffer some disagreeable treatments to get rid of our nasal trouble but it will be well worth it. I had to have an operation on my nose or in my nose and perhaps that is what you need.

In addition to the suggestions I have already made, let me prescribe this course: first, go to Dr. Eastland and have him treat your nose until your head is cleared out. Don't stop until that is done. Then have him decide whether some sort of an operation is necessary or not. If none is needed, then it seems to me the matter falls back on you to make a careful study of your own case and to avoid to the best of our knowledge and ability everything that you have a suspicion that could bring on your troubles.

Lastly when you get a cold in spite of all your care which will happen, then go at once to Dr. Eastland and have him treat your nose until you are clear of cold. Don't think this is a needless expense for it is not. To let your colds drag as yours have in the past is only to incur expense, trouble and disaster for the future…When you feel yourself slipping from your resolutions, and I know you make them, read over some of these suggestions. They are the result of years of experience and a knowledge of your needs and welfare that you perhaps at this time do not fully realize.

With love, Papa

[Editor's note: *Frank was especially interested in avoiding colds and had thoughtfully worked out a plan of action, as set out above, for himself and his children. In his mind, the alternative was disaster. We do not know what type of rhinoplasty surgery Frank had to improve his breathing or avoid the effects of colds.*]

February 8, 1928 (Wednesday)

Dear Sweetheart

After my two hour seminar from 2-4 this afternoon, feeling the need of some fresh air I walked up to the post office found your letter and then walked up to the lake which recent rains have filled up pretty well. The waves are sloshing under the boat house. Quite a number of students were out in boats.

My check came in quite promptly on the 3rd and it was appreciated as my exchequer was getting somewhat depleted. I will divide with you...

I am liking my new rooming place very much better than the first one. [Now] I am pretty well isolated. [In my first place] the landlady's bedroom was next to mine with the bed against my wall. She could out-snore Clarence or Francis without half-trying. I do not know how to describe those sounds—probably it sounded somewhat like a snoring hippopotamus basking in the sun on the muddy banks of a turgid river in tropical Africa. My room instead of being a chamber of peace and slumber at night became a chamber of horrors on several nights. But all that is past.

I have a quiet room, [an] electric stove in my room and bathroom which opens into my room, as well as into the hall. My stove is not one of those circular radiating electric stoves but looks somewhat like an electric toaster, only of course larger...

Lovingly, Frank

February 12, 1928 (Sunday)

Dearest Josie,

When I "take out" or "unhitch" in the evenings and start for town I have three things to make me cheerful. First I have received a letter from home or am expecting one soon, secondly I know I am going to have something good to eat when I come to the end of my walk, and thirdly I have a comfortable room where I can rest and get ready for another day.

I am liking living in town much better than in the dormitory. When I used to leave town in the evening and walk out through the woods or return in the darkness and solitude, a sort of feeling of depression would get hold of me. I don't experience that with my present program. I get my supper at the Mandarin, then leisurely go to my room, enjoying the shop windows as I go...

Glad to know the chickens are picking up. It might be well to lock the back gate. I usually kept it locked. The keys are on top of the mantel...

For the past few summers the papers were full of "Aimee" McPherson, now it is the Hickman trial with all its harrowing details...

I still keep up my walking. Sometimes I am invited two or three times to ride but usually decline with thanks. One morning this week as I walked along the palm drive I saw a lady busily struggling with a tire that was ...reluctant to leave the wheel for her. I soon had it off and the extra to take its place, but she was game and insisted that she could put the nuts on, so accepting her profuse thanks, I hurried on to breakfast.

Concerning the thesis I suppose I can say that progress is being made about as well as can be expected. As for the epidemic it seems to have died down. No new cases this week. But I think I am immune at my age....

With love to all, Frank

[Editor's note: Frank is referring to the infantile paralysis (polio) epidemic. The Hickman case was a gruesome California kidnapping and murder case in

which the defendant made an unsuccessful insanity defense, was found guilty, and hanged at San Quentin in October 1928.]

February 15, 1928 (Wednesday)

Dear Sweetheart,

I have all my valentines displayed in attractive style in my room. Last Sunday for the sake of variety I put on my golf-ball tie and went down to San Jose to hear Rev. John Roach Straton preach. You know he is one of Frank Norris' pals. He is trading pulpits with the pastor of the 1st Church of San Jose for a series of meetings. You know he and his wife and I boarded together at the Willises some twenty years ago. He preached a "powful" sermon or I should say a real good sermon, nothing radical about it…I went up after the sermon and spoke to both the Dr. and Mrs. Straton. I don't think they really remembered me although they politely said they did. She came to Waco as a bride that year and of course was excusable and he usually went around with his head up in the air oblivious of most mortals.

He had a very responsive audience at San Jose…The audience broke out frequently with "amens," "yes yes," "uh huh"—both men and women.

I got back for late dinner and spent the usual Sunday afternoon in the library. If I do not happen to write, don't think I am sick, but rather that the ox is in the ditch.

With love, Frank

[Editor's note: The golf ball tie might have been the only tie Frank took to Palo Alto in 1928, as he occasionally refers to it and to no other.]

[Editor's note on President Brooks' battles: John Roach Straton and Frank Guittard had both been Baylor faculty members together for a couple of years during the early 1900s. President Brooks had hired both Straton and Frank. Straton taught rhetoric at Baylor circa 1903-1905. Straton's classroom or office was close to Frank's on the same floor of the Main Building, called "Old Main" today. He and J. Frank Norris, also a talented speaker and debater, apparently became friends while Norris was a student at Baylor and probably a student of Straton's.

After leaving Baylor, Straton, a gifted speaker, debater, and pulpiteer, became one of a number of fundamentalist preachers in the second and third decades of the 20th century who gained notoriety condemning liberalism, modernism, and German Rationalism in Christian seminaries and churches across the United States. Defining these "isms" is beyond the scope of this volume. Straton and other fundamentalists urged the return to a literal interpretation of the Bible while censuring the teaching of evolution. One of Straton's noted pastorates was in Manhattan where he excelled at unusual ways of drawing attention to himself, his ministry, and his premillennialist message. Straton was an interesting character about whom more will be said in The Life & Times.

Frank Guittard also boarded at the Willis boarding house with Straton and Straton's wife, which would have been circa 1903-1905.]

February 19, 1928 (Sunday)

Dear Sweetheart,

I received a telegram from Francis about his debates…Give my congratulations to Francis for his successes as well as his defeats, for one is about as beneficial in the long run as the other…

I was walking by that little stretch of park near the station the other day and saw the keeper on his knees with a knife going after the dandelions. My sympathy went out to him immediately and I stopped to talk with him. He said the only way to get rid of them was to go after them. I wondered how our dandelions were doing…

With much love, Frank

February 20, 1928 (Monday)

My dear Sweetheart,

Evidently if you have not received a letter in over a week, Uncle Sam is at fault or you must have miscalculated for I am dead sure I have written at least twice every week since I have been here. Once more don't think I am sick, think of a hundred other things that could prevent a letter from crossing the continent. I am as well as I ever have been. I made the trip to the University...four times today. It is called a mile and a quarter but to my place it is easy a mile and a half...The epidemic was reported worse than it really was. I did not hear of anyone eating out of paper platters or drinking cups nor did I see anything of the kind...

I have a race with the Sunset Limited every morning to see who passes the station first. I came out ahead three times last week. It passes at 7:30 you know. It gives me a twinge of homesickness when I think that it came right straight from Texas...

Lovingly, Frank

[Editor's note: The epidemic in California was presumably infantile paralysis (polio).]

February 22, 1928 (Wednesday)

Dear Clarence,

As this was holiday at the University today, all the flags were flying from those tall staffs on the campus. It was a pretty sight…You wrote a good account of your trip to Dallas. Then your penmanship is improving too. I hope you are learning the muscular movement. It is very necessary. I sometimes write for most of the time during some days and if I did not use the muscular movement, I would get very tired but I never do. You seem to be starting right in history. If you keep it up you ought to be a good historian.

I must tell you about a jolly time I had with some dogs last Sunday morning. I started out for my walk before breakfast. Not far from my place two dogs came out to the walk to greet me. I stopped and petted them and when I continued my walk they followed me. I encourage them to do so. One was a police dog, the other was an Airedale. They rollicked with each other as we went along out University Ave. Soon we were joined by an aristocratic looking bulldog and a fine fox terrier. All soon became good friends. It was a little early and I suppose they had gotten tired waiting for their folks to get up so they all came right along with me. It was a jolly bunch of pooches.

You should have seen them walking over the nice lawns we came to. It was a special delight for them when we came to vacant lots which are now overgrown with green wild oats about a foot and a half height, to streak through it and tumble around over each other. They would come out dripping wet as there was heavy dew. At one place the fox terrier jumped up on a low fence covered with a mass of what looked like dead honeysuckle and began to roll around to dry himself. The others soon followed and tried the same stunt. We came to a large sand pile along the walk where a house was under construction. The police dog bounded to the top of it and all the others followed of course. They began to dig holes in the sand just lie boys. They would poke their noses in the holes and pretend they scented some game.

Of the four the police dog was the most obedient. When they would go too far astray a whistle would call him back and the others would soon follow. They stayed with me until I came back to the Snow White Creamery when I said goodbye and we all went our separate ways.

Don't forget about writing that account of a day at school.

With love, Papa

[Editor's note: We have been unable to locate the letter Frank requested Clarence to write. We do remember Clarence explaining to his children, including the editor, how he (Clarence) used the "muscular movement when [he] wrote by hand."]

February 26, 1928 (Sunday morning)

Dear Sweetheart,

Things are moving rather evenly here these days. In fact it is a sort of monotonous strenuosity...I certainly would keep your servant. You would have to have some cleaning and washing done as well... We will come out all right...

Yes, I think it would be a good plan for Francis to take voice but surely not give up the piano after all these years. He ought to practice enough to keep in pretty good trim for playing and especially practice sight reading...How is the garden? How are the flowers? How are the trees? How are the chickens? How are you all?

With love for all, Frank

[Editor's note on President Brooks' battles: By this date, if not before, it was completely clear that the effort to relocate Baylor to Dallas was serious. The Baptists pushing for relocation proposed to raise $1.5 million cash and put up 1,000 acres of land.

President Brooks openly opposed the move for a number of reasons, including the following three: Firstly, Brooks asserted that Baylor and the Baylor-Waco town and gown relationship could not be replicated in Dallas. Four decades of partnership had already been established, including contributions of cash and land, among the city of Waco, its citizens, and Baylor. Secondly, the suggested move would work a hardship on Baylor faculty members as they sought to find new homes in Dallas. Such a trial might lead some to abandon Baylor for other universities making better offers.

Thirdly, relocation would alienate a substantial number of Baylor (at Waco) alumni who had spent a significant amount of time in Waco, before and after graduation. Additionally, contributions made by Wacoans had allowed Baylor to secure a matching amount from the General Education Fund of the Rockefeller Foundation.

Lastly, an additional reason for opposing a move to Dallas was that angering donors who had made significant gifts to Baylor athletics would hinder recruitment of outstanding local high school athletes. These included players on the 1927 Waco High School championship team coached by Paul Tyson. Tyson was the most successful high school football coach of the 1920s and Tyson's Waco Tigers won four state football championships in the 1920s (1922, 1925, 1926, and 1927). In 1927 the Tigers outscored their opponents 782 to 33 and boasted a 14-0 record. Moreover, the 1927 team was recognized unofficially as the national high school championship team after defeating an outstanding team from Cleveland, Ohio 40 to 14.]

February 29, 1928 (Wednesday night)

Dear Sweetheart,

What you write about the Stratons clears up something I did not understand. I talked to Mrs. Straton while the Doctor was greeting the line and then fell in as one of the last in the line. Since neither one said anything about having been in Texas I asked each one pointedly whether they were going through Texas on their way home. As I remember now each one assumed a sort of mysterious expression of countenance and evaded my question.

[Regarding Herbert Hoover] It was remarked by the wife of one of the professors here and I suppose she ought to know, that Hoover had an awful time passing his Freshman English. He, of course, specialized in engineering. It proves that a man may fall down in one line and still have marked ability in other lines.

If I were not a Democrat, I think I would favor Hoover. As it is I do not see much to arouse the enthusiasm in any of the proposed Democratic candidates. I believe that Smith would get the largest vote but doubt whether he would get enough to be elected. The Democratic Party seems to be gradually losing ground. Lack of unity and lack of success in national elections has done much to cause a falling off of numbers or better perhaps lack of increase in number of adherents. When a young man casts his first vote if he has no strong convictions, he wants his vote to count and that makes him a Republican in many states. I think this is one great reason for the decline of the Democrats. It is difficult to get up any enthusiasm for a cause that is almost sure to fail...

I haven't talked politics with anyone for some time and since I have relieved myself, I shall turn in for the night.

With love, Frank

March 4, 1928 (Sunday morning)

Dearest Josie,

I do not sleep very often in church these days or Sundays. If Dr. Dawson ever disturbs my slumbers like he did the man's you write about, I shall be inclined to think I can dispense with his preaching for when I get sleepy it a sign that I have been paying him the decided compliment of attention. I never get sleepy when my mind is wandering here and there. The secret of my reading at night is to get my mind fixed on something so I can sleep....

Yes, I am still liking my new room. They keep the room very nice even wash my drinking glass which our servant at home would generally manage to forget.

About the dog: I suppose it would be better to let Clarence have one and be done with it. I would not like to have him feel like [the son of another faculty member] when he grows to manhood that his parents had denied him the great joy of childhood—having a "purp" to lick his face, etc. I would suggest however to get a short haired one. The flea and laundry problems are sufficient even at that. My greatest objection to having a dog around children has been removed—the danger of rabies. And of course have him vaccinated.

With love for all, Frank.

March 7, 1928 (Wednesday)

Dearest Josie,

Glad to know you settled with the income tax collector...I think the income tax was some less than last year. You must have induced the collector to give all the exemptions possible. I shall feel like having you see the collector next year...

I have told you about all there is to tell...about the thesis which still is in an indefinite state of progress. I hope to have some limits for it before a great while. This all sounds very mysterious I know. Don't imagine ...that I am not doing any work... for quite the contrary is the case. I haunt the library. I am becoming an intimate acquaintance with all the library force from the top to the lower regions where the old musty newspaper files are stored for those who wish to dig up the records of the past...

With much love, Frank

March 11, 1928 (Sunday)

Dear Francis,

I think your program for the next quarter is a good one. Glad to know that you intend to keep up your piano practice. You must be making some progress in vocal to be able to take part in vocal quartette renditions. Also glad to know that you are going to try to break [Harold] Knop's monopoly on the Connally debate. I think you ought to run him a pretty close race...

The time has come when you should begin to plan definitely for your work after you get through school and not leave it to chance or the urge of conditions at the time, which has been the bane of my life. There is no reason in your case why you cannot lay out a definite plan and bend everything toward it.

Your summers in Colorado have done much for you physically but I somewhat doubt whether it would be wise to continue them. If you cannot get a place that is really worthwhile, I think it would be much better to spend those four months at something that would fit you along the line of your law work. So I suggest this for the summer: Four months at your age and period of preparation mean a great deal and should not be frittered away. You of course want to make a success of law and want to get into practice as soon as possible. There is no reason why you should not make a success of it if you go at in the right way and keep at it.

I think the first thing for you to do is to prepare to make yourself useful in some law office. It is useless to think of "hanging out your shingle" independently. To prepare yourself for such a place, the first requirement of course is your knowledge of law; second, you should be a proficient typist; third, an expert stenographer; and fourth, you should have some knowledge of accounting.

So I think it would pay you to work along this line this summer rather than to go to Colorado if you cannot get a place very much better than any you have had up to this time. Don't "piddle around" trying to become an expert along these lines by private study. It won't be done. It will become a side issue. I wish you would investigate Toby's, the C.C.C. School and Baylor and let me know what a scholarships or tuition would be for these lines of study and let me know soon. Remember those four months are going to mean a great deal for you future. There will be a hundred lawyers who will have perhaps as much legal ability as you but they will not have these other advantages…

Lovingly, Papa

[Editor's note: Toby's was a business school in Waco that taught office skills like book-keeping, stenography, and typing. It also fielded a football team which sometimes played against college teams like Baylor. Francis became a reasonably proficient typist by the time he obtained a position with a law firm.

The C.C.C. School was obviously not the Civilian Conservation Corps for unemployed, unmarried men initiated by President Franklin Roosevelt in 1933. It was probably a school offering correspondence courses in practical subjects like stenography and typing that Frank thought would be useful for Francis as a fledgling attorney at a law firm.

Clarence, on the other hand, who also went into the law, was not as fortunate with his efforts to develop typing proficiency, telling one of his children that his fingers didn't seem to do what they were supposed to do. Apparently lacking average manual dexterity, he reportedly dropped a typing course, probably in high school, to avoid a failing grade. Years later, however, after he no longer had access to a legal secretary but had a computer word processor, he managed to generate many documents in connection with his bar association committee work. We do not know whether he was able to draw upon a residue of his typing training in high school or just had to hunt and peck.]

March 14, 1928 (Wednesday night)

Dear Sweetheart,

I hope you can send something to Wood Brothers. I have the Shaffer bill about paid off. We are coming through slowly but surely I hope...

I could not have undertaken this task in the world if it had not been for you...You have been as good and sweet as can be about writing. One thing, you have not written anything to worry me. I hope you will continue to keep all worries from me as I need all time and attention for my work. You know it does not take much to make my spirits rise or fall. I usually try to keep cheerful but it is hard sometimes.

If Francis continues to have trouble with his eyes, have him try my remedy. A few weeks ago my eyes began to feel scratchy as a result of reading papers with poor print and also German...I heated some water moderately hot, saturated the end of a towel and held this on my eyes for five or ten minutes, reheating it of course each night after finishing my study. It gave me almost immediate relief...

The other evening as I was coming out the "Grill," two couples get out of a car and started for the restaurant. All were smoking cigarettes. One of the girls removed her cigarette from her very ruby lips, held it daintily between her two fingers, tilted her head up and a little to one side, and shot a streak of smoke very expertly into the atmosphere. As they entered the door I heard her say to the other girl, "Let's not get any darn clam chowder or roast beef." When I enter the restaurants sometimes I am inspired with somewhat similar sentiments.

Lovingly, Frank

[Editor's note: Wood Brothers and Shaffer's were stores in Waco selling men's clothing.]

[Editor's note on President Brooks' battles: It is not clear whether Josie ever tried to shield Frank from news about the movement to relocate Baylor to Dallas. Frank's letters to her later on make it clear he kept up-to-date on

developments back in Texas, although there was a significant time-lag for the delivery of mail to California. As previously noted, such news stories would have been worrisome to Frank who was 61 years of age and deep into his studies at Stanford. He could not afford to spend time worrying about a possible move to Dallas.]

March 18, 1928 (Sunday)

Dear Clarence,

I hope you received those reminders of the Palo Alto tree and the copy of the story of it as well as your book.

As I pretend to be a law-abiding citizen, I was somewhat careful when I poached those samples. They have a very nice looking jail here on the outside but I am not sure about the accommodations on the inside and then I would not care to look out through iron bars. So I was careful to stand the big tree between me and the park attendant while I got your samples. Sure you can use the Shenandoah relics. I know you will be careful with them...

I saw a real animal story enacted the other morning. I had just walked through that low place in front of the University which is partly planted in shrubbery...when I heard a dog yelping very excitedly. I was standing near the front of the University building and could see a black and white bird dog in full chase after a jack-rabbit. The rabbit ran for that shrubbery and when he was nearly through it, he made a sudden turn to the right, almost a right angle. The dog kept on straight ahead and of course lost his trail. He ran about whining and in great distress but could not find the trail again, while Mr. Rabbit was leisurely hopping away down toward the Arbovitum, wagging his ears back and forward and with a broad smile on his face.

Lovingly, Papa

[Editor's note: Frank was probably referring to the Stanford University Arboretum in the last sentence.]

March 21, 1928 (Wednesday night)

Dearest Josie,

Will I be home in June? No, indeed, my dear. I hope I have not ever left the impression that I would, for there is not the least possibility of it… Most students stay longer than the two years after receiving their Master's Degree. I will not have been here two years by June. I am just an ordinary hard worker and not a genius.

I wonder if you realize what a task I have before me. …it almost overwhelms me [to think of it] and I get terribly blue and discouraged and wonder whether after all it is worthwhile. I don't dare to think much about it. I just try to take as big a nibble from the base of the mountains each day without trying to look over, around, or through them…

Of course it would be a great pleasure for several reasons to go to Houston. I think your [sic] wrote some time ago that the Bryans are going. I would like for you to go with them, since I cannot go to help nominate Smith…

There is one thing however that I should like to say about planning for next summer. I do not think I could unreservedly give my consent to have Clarence come out here again. It was hard to do so last summer and only [given] because plans had been made and I knew what a great disappointment it would be to both of you and then to me too not to have you make the trip. Perhaps I am over-cautious but I think perhaps I have had enough in the past to make it excusable in me for being so. I was in a more or less state of anxiety all the time he was here. The doctors with whom I consulted said they had the trouble here every summer…

Now something for home consumption strictly. I have taken my examination in French and passed. I ate up a French grammar and devoured a heap of French history without getting indigestion, but it did get on my nerves somewhat; however, I am rapidly recovering. The evening after I learned I had passed, I dined at the "Cardinal" to celebrate the event, then [too] I was somewhat curious too as to whether I would know how to act after spending so much time in Chinese restaurants and cafeterias for the past three months. I think I performed all right with the shrimp, fork, salad fork, artichoke finger-bowl, and other accessories.

More for home consumption if you are not "fed up": my thesis subject is settled as far as I know...What is before me? First, the examination in German which will be a steep hill to climb. The French exam was no farce or sham or pretense. It was a written test on some stuff I had never seen. I think I know French better than German. So I have some work to do in German. Second, the final oral examination and preparation in nine fields. This is more than a steep hill. It is a real mountain, a Matterhorn. Third, the completion of the thesis. This is almost a Mount Everest. ... It is not the most cheerful kind of prospect....

This week is examination week, but I shall have none, but it does not relieve me much. Next week will be vacation, all week. However, there will be no vacation for this guy or bird or digger.

The weather now is much like in summer. For three weeks I have laid aside my overcoat and put away my woolen sox. It is chilly mornings and evenings but that is when I do my brisk walking and I soon warm up.

Love to all, Frank

[Editor's note: When Frank talked about his being cautious where serious health matters were involved, he was obviously thinking about the son (Charles) he believed he lost to infectious disease, infantile paralysis or spinal meningitis in 1916, and the wife (Mamie) he lost in 1917 to tuberculosis. However, based on the records we have and other available evidence, Charles' infectious disease was likely tubercular meningitis which he developed from exposure to his mother Mamie who died the next year in a tuberculosis sanatorium in Albuquerque.

The "Cardinal" restaurant he is apparently referring to was a restaurant at the Cardinal Hotel in Palo Alto.]

March 25, 1928 (Sunday)

Dearest Josie,

I have made my three walks daily in spite of the rain... Mr. Belk says he very seldom gets an invitation [to ride]... I tell him he does not put on enough dignity.

Nearly every morning when I come to the Union one of the old fellows who sweeps up the leaves around the place takes "time out," spits some "ambier-petunah!!"—then says, "Good morning, professor-r-r."...

I am glad you were able to reestablish our credit at Wood Bros. We are pulling through gradually.

One of my correspondence students...wrote me that he had fallen in his airplane and had not been able to do much on his course lately as he had his leg broken and was otherwise bruised up. I told him he was entitled to a "lay off."

Lovingly, "The Digger"

[Editor's note: Frank frequently received invitations to ride to or from the university but generally turned them down. Frank was unusually dignified in the opinion of his history students at Baylor.]

March 28, 1928 (Wednesday)

Dear Sonny Boy,

I am glad to see by your grades in music that you are keeping up with it. I know you will have some good pieces to play when I get home. I got my grades today. They are all A's and of course I am glad because they are the last ones to put down on my record.

What kind of pooch have you? Has he any sense? What is his name? How is he marked: Is his tail long or short? How did you come to get him? Why not write me something about him? Is he a lovely dog? Does he like to lick your face?

Lovingly, Papa

[Editor's note: Frank received the last of the letter grades to go on his permanent school record at age 61. Frank's intent in making this comment was probably didactic and for the benefit of eleven-year-old Clarence.]

April 1, 1928 (Sunday)

Dear Sweetheart,

I think you did the proper thing in having your [rent house] fitted out with an indoor toilet. I hope you had connections put in for a bath too for that will probably be the next requirement. Then when I get through my vacation job, if I ever will, I will give the house a coat of paint…

I am enclosing the grades of the boys. Francis' B in music and the demerits do not look very good. I suppose there is some good explanation for both…

Registration comes tomorrow. I register for one course History 240—Graduate Research—which means thesis. I suppose the tuition will be $60 as usual.

As to the publication of the thesis, I think that is a voluntary matter. But there is an abundance of time to consider that question. I do not know yet whether I ever shall have one at all.

Our rainy season still continues—rained all last night.

Lovingly, Frank

[Editor's note: By "vacation job," Frank was sarcastically referring to his work on his dissertation, undoubtedly again responding indirectly to those in Waco who might suggest to Josie he was on holiday in Palo Alto.]

April 4, 1928 (Wednesday night)

Dear Sweetheart,

When you are sure of that interesting news about Miss Tanner, I wish you would let me know for I have some plans for Guy...

Glad to hear Francis was successful in the Rice debate.

Lovingly, Frank

[Editor's note: Guy B. Harrison, Jr. was one of Frank's student graders at Baylor and a favorite protégé. He became both a member of Baylor's history faculty and the Director of The Texas Collection for many years. Aleph Tanner was also a member of the history department at Baylor and the first curator of The Texas Collection.]

[Editor's note on President Brooks' battles: According to the Baylor Lariat on April 4, which Frank would not have received from Josie until maybe a week later, the Waco community's counter offer to the proposed move to relocate Baylor to Dallas had now emerged. Waco was willing to fight with promises of dollars and not just words to keep Baylor and its faculty in Waco. The Waco Chamber of Commerce promised the following new additions to the Baylor campus in Waco: a new auditorium (Waco Hall), a new woman's dormitory (Woman's Memorial Dormitory), and a new stadium for athletics. Frank and Josie would have been greatly encouraged that the relocation threat was not only meeting stiff resistance, but possibly going to result in a positive changes for Baylor.

Of course, the relocation battle was not over yet; there was still considerable uncertainty about its outcome. After all, the Seventy-Five Million Campaign waged by Southern Baptists (1919-1924) to benefit Southern Baptist institutions had not been completely successful, raising only $58 million of the $92 million pledged.

The reasons for the failure of the aforementioned campaign include the 1920 recession as well as the tendency on the part of some Baptist agencies to be overly optimistic when it came to budgeting. Frank would have been very aware of the campaign's failure to reach its goal and the reasons why. In a later letter, Frank will offer his own ideas on how a university could best raise large sums, such ideas drawn from his familiarity with fund raising approaches observed while a student at the University of Chicago between 1897 and 1902.

Frank would also have been aware that J. Frank Norris was still out there, stoking distrust of, and anger with, Baylor University, and with big campaigns intended to raise money for Baylor University and other institutions. Norris reportedly only contributed $100 towards rebuilding Carroll Library and Chapel at Baylor after the catastrophic fire in 1922. Norris certainly could not be relied on to help raise money for additions to the Baylor campus or to help President Brooks, an arch-enemy.]

April 8, 1928 (Sunday)

Dear Francis,

I attended two debates this week in order to be able to give you some idea of the status of debating out here. [Here Frank provided a detailed critique of two debates involving Stanford teams and teams from Manila University] Comparing the debaters with Baylor speakers and debaters, I think they are not superior but if you should come out here next year, you will find some keen fellows to oppose you...

How are you progressing with your vocal and public speaking? You have been a student long enough to realize that the more a student puts into a course himself, the more he gets out of it. The little time spent in the class is only a small part of the work. It is much more the case with music and public speaking...

That proposition you mention as having been proposed by Dr. Brooks sounds pretty good for one reason especially, it would give you development along the line of your future work. As to the financial part of the summer program, if that is necessary, I think that can be taken care of.

Lovingly, Papa

[Editor's note: It sounds like Frank and Francis had been corresponding regarding the idea of Francis joining his father in Palo Alto and taking summer courses that would have benefited someone aspiring to be a lawyer, presumably along the lines of practical courses of the type mentioned in Frank's later letter of May 13, 1928 hereinafter.]

April 9, 1928 (Monday night)

Dear Papa,

My pooch is a fox terrier. He has more sense than Sam did. He is a pretty smart dog. His name is William Barrett Travis, Billy for short. Billy's tail is long. When I was sick, Mamma Josie got him at the veterinarian's....He does not like to lick face...

With love, Clarence

[Editor's note: It would be interesting to know who named "Billy." It certainly could have been Clarence who was eleven at the time of this letter and already would have heard or read basic Texas history.]

April 11, 1928 (Wednesday)

Dear Sweetheart,

Those articles in the papers are very interesting but after reading them there is a great big question mark before me, namely, where is Waco going to get all the money to erect those new buildings?...

I did not receive my salary check until yesterday, the 10th as it was addressed to "Stanford, Calif." It must have been held up somewhere. I have written Hudson and I suppose it will not occur again. If I had not kept a reserve, I might have been placed in an embarrassing situation...I am also sending you the balance of the Shaffer's bill which you may mail to him. He has been sending me the statement until this month. I thought perhaps you might have paid the bill because I did not hear from him this month...I think we can clean up next month. Let me know how much is still due on the Halsey and Wood Bills.

It is awfully nice of you to keep writing so often.

With love and a kiss, Frank

[Editor's note on President Brooks' battles: Frank at the beginning of the letter is apparently referring to newspaper articles, including the Baylor Lariat from a week earlier, discussing the proposal that several buildings be added to the Baylor campus in Waco, including a new auditorium or chapel, a new athletic stadium, and a new woman's dormitory. The proposal for these new buildings was part of the drive to keep Baylor in Waco.]

April 15, 1928 (Sunday morning)

Dearest Josie,

The sox especially were appreciated. I walk so much that they do not last very long. I hope the fruit escaped the frost during the recent cold spell.

Things are grinding along as usual mostly. I do not know whether my adviser is apprehensive that I am going to get through too soon or whether he is desirous that I should finish up in the right way. He suggested that I "sit in" on two courses this quarter, that is, not sign up for the courses with a view of getting credit but get the lectures & bibliography. I regarded the suggestion as a sort of requirement and, as he has been very kind and helpful, I followed the suggestion. One course is in Chinese History-"Chinese Civilization," the other Historiography, which means the history of history. I find both very interesting.

Dr. Martin has the course in Historiography. He wanted me to enroll and become an active member of the class. He presented me to the class or seminar, numbering eight or ten, saying I was head of the History Department of Baylor University, away on a leave of absence. He also added that he hoped I would become a real member of the class, not so much for what I would get out of the work, but for what I would contribute to it. I of course expressed my appreciation...but had a talk with him afterward and will continue with the class as an "auditor," although he said he would like for me to take an active part in the discussions. These two courses will mean five class hours a week and some reading to get any real benefit from the work, but I have found that it is best to follow suggestions.

I suppose you read Al's letter. Don't be alarmed--I am not thinking of starting for the Philippines very soon or sending any money to precede my journey. Al seems to think I am blessed with ready cash. He of course does not know that I have several bills waiting patiently or perhaps impatiently in my drawer right now.

Lovingly, Frank

[Editor's note: We do not know how much money Frank's older brother Alwin Guittard, a physician in the Philippines, wanted to borrow from Frank. We suspect he may have thought Frank was flush with money because Mamie, his deceased first wife, had a banker father. Perhaps he did not realize that Mamie's and her mother's estates provided only for Francis and Clarence, not Frank.]

April 18, 1928 (Wednesday night)

Dearest Josie,

You must have had a presentiment that this was a day for celebrating. The box came this morning and I got it at noon when I came home for dinner. Why am I celebrating? Well I have something for home consumption strictly: I took my German examination and P-A-S-S-E-D!

Aufwiedersehen...to German. *Au revoir* to German. *Pax vobiscum*—Peace be with you—the German

Aufwiedersehen to my German friends of the past few weeks with whom I have gotten pretty well acquainted. Mommsen, Lambrechts, Treitschke, Sybel, Otto von Bismarck, Hedwig von Bismarck (Otto's Frau), Emil Ludwig, Jastrow—to all—*pax vobiscum*...most of them are good enough people but the sentential structure of most [of] them lacks terminal facilities.

If I had read German history much longer, I think I should have become either a misanthrope, or a cynic or a pessimist of the extremest type....It all hung over me like a lowering cloud. *Jetzt ist es weg fur ewig*! (now gone forever).

I did not want to be selfish so I invited the Belks to celebrate with me at the Sunset Cafeteria. The little boy has a severe cold again so I had a party of one at "the Cardinal." ...

Next Monday night the Department of History [Dr. Robinson] gives an "at home" to its graduate students...A tuxedo will not be necessary. If all the others sport theirs, I shall feel perfectly at home with my Shaffer suit—which is paid for—and my golf-ball tie....

After my ordeal with German is over and I look back over some of my college work, I feel a bit resentful at the way in which I was taught German and I might say also the way it is taught at present. Reading easy stories, poetry, and plays is a very inadequate preparation for anyone who expects to do anything with German history. I had to learn practically a new vocabulary when I came to the reading of history...The most interesting thing I read was

Ludwig's *Life of Napoleon*. He [Ludwig] has gotten away from the involved sentences of older writers…

Well, I feel terribly relieved.

Lovingly, Frank

[Editor's note: Frank's practice of telling Josie that bits of information he disclosed to her were for "home consumption" could have been based on a number of things, but we suspect that he was loathe primarily to make statements that could be perceived back at Baylor as bragging, or, worst case, that he might have to take back for some reason.

His reference to wearing his "golf-ball" tie with his newish suit seems to be a joke between him and Josie, and this is the second letter in which he has referred to wearing this tie on a semi-formal occasion.]

April 22, 1928 (Sunday)

Dear Sweetheart,

Since I worked at such high tension for a number of weeks to get those language examinations off my mind, I find that after it is over... I am suffering from an attack of a feeling very much akin to laziness at times. The old philosophers held to the theory that the world is governed by two opposing forces such as light and darkness, good and evil, active and passive, industry and indolence, etc. and that man himself is a good illustration of this theory and sometimes it is doubtful which side will win. For a half day at least after my German examination I let indolence prevail. I did nothing but write letters, catch up with my correspondence work, and so some thinking and planning for the next campaign. Thursday morning Mr. Will had some difficulty in whipping me in line again. He is certainly a slave driver. But I am stepping along about as usual with the whip popping over my head occasionally as a gentle reminder that there is to be no letup in this matter...

How is the Buick holding up? Have you given it a dose of polish yet?

With much love, Frank. I am still eating home-made candy.

[Editor's note: Frank's general view seemed to be that there were only two ways to spend one's time: the first was to work "in earnest," and the second was simply to fritter one's time away.]

April 25, 1928 (Wednesday night)

Dear Sweetheart,

You were unusually nice about writing and sending papers last week I was interested in all of the news. However, I cannot yet understand why the Chamber of Commerce could expect to accomplish anything by having a "speeler" make such unfounded statements about what Waco was going to do. Surely they know it could not in the end help matters but real be a detriment to any real effort to do something...

[Frank]

*[Editor's note on President Brooks' battles: We do not know what "speeler"
Frank is referring to. His comment in part may indicate Frank's life-long
disdain of making unfounded comments.]*

April 29, 1928 (Sunday morning)

Dear Sweetheart,

I think the alumni are right in asserting their views...I still think Baylor could not afford to move for less than five million [dollars] and even then there are certain elements that would make the move of doubtful advantage.

Are the examinations ahead easier than the language exams? I should say not. ... I am now facing an examination in nine different fields of history, must know the bibliography of each field, as well as knowing the history; besides I am required to know all about Historical Method, Research, and weighing of historical evidence added to this...I am almost afraid to go to my conferences for fear something more will be heaped upon me.

I have become an abject slave. Can you imagine yourself studying eight hours a day, day after day, week after week. I refuse to study Sunday night. That is my only rest time...

The campus these days looks like a great hay field. The wild oats was cut, and after it was dry, raked up and stacked in small heaps...I suppose [it] will be baled. The smell of new hay reminded me of old farm days...I saw some ripe cherries on a tree this morning.

Lovingly, "The Digger"

[Editor's note on President Brooks' battles: The alumni's views Frank is referring to were overwhelmingly in favor of Baylor remaining in Waco, with the strong feeling that it was simply impossible to remove Baylor from Waco and transplant it in Dallas.

Nevertheless, on April 29, 1928, at a meeting of the Education Commission of the Baptist General Convention of Texas, George W. Truett and twelve other commission members voted to move Baylor to Dallas, notwithstanding the sixteen reasons former Texas Governor Pat Neff presented as to why Baylor should not be moved to Dallas. Only O.S. Lattimore joined Neff in the vote to keep Baylor in Waco. Frank, as of the date of this letter, and possibly the next, had clearly not heard of this meeting or its decision.]

[Editor's note: This letter contains at least the third instance of Frank using the term "digger" to vividly convey his perspective on his slavish task. No doubt he could have used more colorful terms if he had had a mind to. The following letter uses the phrase "digging, digging."]

May 2, 1928 (Wednesday night)

Dear Sweetheart,

I have … paid my church subscription up to date so you can look everybody square [in the eye] in the fall when you meet them. I am still digging, digging...

[The book lists for History courses] 224 & 217 might be in my desk drawer in my recitation room or in the middle drawer of my office desk…

Lovingly, Frank.

[Editor's note: Frank may or may not have been joking about looking "everybody square [in the eye]," but probably not about having to catch up on his subscription. Josie in particular could have been sensitive on this topic. Information about subscriptions may not have been completely confidential to the deacons and church treasurer.

Frank's reference to his classroom as his "recitation room" tracks with his teaching style, which was basically a modified recitation style by which he questioned his students over their reading assignments.]

[Editor's note on President Brooks' battles: Regarding what was now being called the Greater Baylor Campaign to keep Baylor in Waco, Frank and Josie must have felt much better about their chances of staying in Waco and continuing their customary lifestyle.

A second proposal, valued at a total of $4,300,000 to keep Baylor in Waco, was now made public, along the following lines: the cities of Waco and Dallas pledged one million dollars apiece. Three new buildings would be erected: Waco Hall, an athletic stadium, and a woman's dormitory. Baylor University committed to raising two million dollars through state-wide fund raising. Lastly, the General Education Board of the Rockefeller Foundation committed to $300,000, on the condition that Baylor pay off approximately $500,000 it owed in debt.]

May 6, 1928 (Sunday morning)

Dear Sweetheart,

Many thanks for the papers. I am with Brooks and Neff on the question. As I look at the matter from this distance, the plan is to concentrate on that special convention. 1st, Waco should have something substantial to offer to counterbalance the Dallas offer. Then if Brooks, Neff and Lattimore can have an opportunity to speak to the convention, it will go a long way. Lattimore I think can get closer to the "brethren" than any other layman in the Convention. However, if Truett casts his spell over the "sistring and brethering" in favor of Dallas it is "all off." Can't Judge Jenkins be persuaded to induce his son-in-law [Truett] to remain neutral? It will all depend on Truett. Arguments will not mean so much to the Convention, both sides have good arguments...

I think someone ought to give the local editor some advice. His editorials on the Baylor situation are childish, puerile, and immature, and quite often rotten...

Lovingly, Frank

[Editor's note on President Brooks' battles: In this letter, Frank is yet unaware that a second and very strong proposal [the 4.3 million dollar proposal] as set out above had already been made on behalf of Baylor remaining in Waco and that the Baylor situation therefore had already taken a favorable turn. He is possibly also not aware, on the other hand, that George W. Truett, pastor of the First Baptist Church in Dallas, had just voted to move Baylor to Dallas. Although Frank and Josie had a telephone, they did not use it to keep in touch, only using letters and a rare telegram. There was often a significant lag time for mail delivery.

Frank had good reason to be concerned about the position Truett might take on the matter. Truett, a Baylor graduate, had been responsible for raising monies to keep Baylor solvent several decades previously and was known from his student days at Baylor for both his prodigious fund raising skills and his preaching prowess, neither of which could be matched by his contemporaries. Truett and Frank Guittard having both been members of the Erisophian Literary Society together in the early 1890s, Frank certainly had first-hand knowledge of Truett's persuasiveness in both speaking and debating.

Further, for three or four decades after graduation from Baylor, Truett was without much dispute the most influential Southern Baptist leader of his generation, and, in fact, was president of the Southern Baptist Convention at the time of this letter. However, Truett was the son-in-law of Judge W.H. Jenkins, an influential member of Baylor's Board of Trustees, who favored keeping Baylor in Waco, which may have mitigated against Truett being completely inflexible on the relocation issue.

John Compere Lattimore was superintendent of the Waco Public School System and a former professor of mathematics and pedagogy at Baylor who had served as chair of the Baylor faculty for two years following the resignation of Rufus C. Burleson in 1897.

Pat M. Neff, a contemporary of Frank Guittard at Baylor who had already served two terms as governor of Texas, became president of Baylor in 1932 after President Brooks' death in 1931. Neff and Brooks had both been members of the Philomathesian Literary Society in the 1890s, the rival society to the Erisophian Literary Society of which Frank and Truett had been members.]

[Editor's note: The literary societies at Baylor were, as mentioned earlier, essentially competitive speaking and debating societies which kept their own small libraries to facilitate their members' debates with the members of the other societies. The literary societies were forerunners of modern college fraternities and sororities.]

May 9, 1928 (Wednesday night)

Dear Sweetheart,

You are very nice and kind to suggest some reading for a time of relaxation but my dear, there is no relaxation for this guy. I wonder sometimes how it would feel to be in a condition or state of mind without anything impending over me, once again…

With much love, Frank

[Editor's note on President Brooks' battles: On May 11, the Dallas Morning News reported that Baylor had rejected the "Dallas" offer to relocate Baylor to Dallas.]

May 13, 1928 (Sunday)

Dear Francis,

I suppose what I meant in my letter is what you term "permanent job." When I said that you should prepare to make yourself useful in a law office I certainly did not mean that you should prepare to be an errand boy. You could have taken a position like that before you entered high school. It states in my two letters that you should prepare to take a position in a law office after you finish your law course. What do I mean by that statement? Simply this: Getting a place as Sims Brooks started with.

I would judge that first you would have to make use of your legal knowledge, making out briefs or helping to prepare cases for trial, making out legal papers and taking charge of minor cases yourself. That would be your law work. Besides that, I said you should be able to do clerical or secretarial work. In other words, be more than a lawyer be an expert in writing and stenography. Then you would some advantage over other young lawyers in competing for a position in a law office with an established firm.

As to what Sam Amsler says about bookkeeping, I am sure he is right when it comes to business hours but I venture to say there are few if any bookkeeping machines in law offices in Waco. But for that matter perhaps you could get a manual on bookkeeping, as I did, and get all the knowledge that you might need. I did not suggest that you should go into a law office until after you finish your law course. [Emphasis supplied by Frank]

Love, Papa

[Editor's note: Sims Brooks was the son of President Samuel Palmer Brooks.
Sam Amsler was a lawyer cousin of Francis' maternal grandmother, Eliza Amsler Welhausen.

Frank Guittard's advice to Francis about how to establish himself in a law office and prepare himself for law practice was well-thought-out and likely formulated over a number of years.]

May 16, 1928 (Wednesday night)

Dear Sweetheart,

I was real glad to get the papers on the Baylor situation. More than glad to see the outcome of it all. The only discordant note is that editorial in the "Times Herald"…He certainly has a narrow conception of a newspaper's function in trying to mold public opinion. A boy of fifteen or less knows that a magnanimous spirit always does more than petty bickering…

You ask about my thesis. Following the suggestion of my adviser, the thesis is on a side-track for the present, waiting for a train on the main line.

Well I have nothing new to write about. Each day passes just like the one before. Some days I go the entire day [without] talking to anyone except a few necessary words to the waiters.

I hope you will not measure my love and appreciation for what you do by the length of my letters.

Lovingly, Frank

P.S. Thank you for the lists and the books.

[Editor's note on President Brooks' battles: Frank in the first paragraph is apparently glad that with recent events, including the initial outpouring of public support for Baylor verbally, if not financially, and the idea of new additions to the Waco campus, the "Dallas" offer to relocate Baylor to Dallas had been rejected and it appeared that the relocation offer was now in doubt, if not doomed. We have not been able to identify which editorial Frank is complaining about, which side it took, or why it offended him.]

May 20, 1928 (Sunday morning)

Dearest Josie,

I suppose the Convention at Waco will not be an occasion for the mere turning loose of pious and benevolent gas. Joe Burt and Lyon and others have indicated there are some men waiting to do something great for Baylor. It seems to me if these fellows have anything back of their talk, this is the time for them to show it. They ought to smoke out these big gifts or admit that they were just relying on their imaginations or just naturally lying.

I think Baylor people in the past have made the wrong sort of an appeal. We are all inherently selfish and vain. Trace man back to the caves. He has always been interested in self and he will be a long time getting away from himself. Of course, there are individual exceptions. Benevolence is a sort of a veneer for men's acts quite often. Get down under that veneer and you will find self and vanity. When you appeal to men to give to endowment for the good of coming generations, they think: well if I give to that fund, it will soon be forgotten whether I gave or did not give and if I do give there will be nothing especially to show for it.

Dr. Harper [president of the University of Chicago] thoroughly understood this fundamental trait of human nature. There is, I believe, not a single building on the campus of the University of Chicago that is not a monument to the generosity of individuals...I heard Dr. Harper give the story of this donation [Yerkes' Astronomical Observatory at Geneva, Wisconsin]. He visited Yerkes the street-car magnate of Chicago in his office. He told him that he wanted him to do something for the University worthy of himself [Yerkes] and that would leave a monument to his name for all time. Yerkes: What do you want me to do? Harper: Make it possible to establish the greatest astronomical observatory in the world. Yerkes: How much will you need? Harper: One million dollars. Without another word Yerkes wrote out his check for a million and handed it to Harper.

That is a sample of the way Dr. Harper made his appeals. It was largely an appeal to vanity and selfishness, to establish a name and to leave an enduring monument...

Lovingly, Frank

[Editor's note on President Brooks' battles: Dr. William Rainey Harper was the first president of the University of Chicago. Harper, along with wealthy patron John D. Rockefeller, who donated record sums to establish the university, was responsible for building the campus and recruiting the faculty. Frank obviously thought that Harper's ideas for raising money from alumni and other backers had merit and hoped that President Brooks and other prominent Baptists would see fit to use them.

Harper was the university president during the periods when Frank was in residence in Chicago working on his A.B. and A.M. degrees. He was also a cornet player like Frank and occasionally would sit in with the University band. It is possible they both played cornet together on some random occasion with the University band.

The editor is convinced that Harper, also from Ohio, and Frank knew each other, but, speculation aside, there is little evidence to support this conclusion other than a photograph published in the Baylor Round-Up of Baylor faculty members and others taken on the steps of Carroll Science Building, showing both Frank and Dr. Harper, and the fact that Dr. Harper was president of the University of Chicago during each of the six periods when Frank attended.]

May 23, 1928 (Wednesday night)

Dear Sweetheart,

It seems to me that if you need a servant at all it is during the summer. There will be little saved when you pay for ironing and cleaning occasionally. So I would say keep your servant. Financially it is not at all necessary for you to do that work and I would rather you would not…

I am at present passing through one of the most trying ordeals of my life and I have had several of them along the years.

Lovingly, Frank

[Editor's note: Frank did not specifically identify "the most trying ordeals" he referred to here. However, two academic or professional ordeals he endured were teaching at an ungraded school at the beginning of his public school teaching career in Texas, and then fifteen years later preparing himself to teach multiple subjects other than history during his first year in Baylor's Preparatory Department.

Frank had other ordeals which were personal, including watching helplessly as his son Charles suffered and succumbed to fatal disease, and then the next year watching wife Mamie suffer from tuberculosis before removal to a sanatorium in Albuquerque where she died a month after arrival.]

May 25, 1928 (Friday) [Western Union Telegram]

[To] FG GUITTARD: WON THE CONNALLY DEBATE PRIZE OF
FIFTY DOLLARS; FRANK WILSON SECOND; KNOP THIRD; SOPHIES
ALSO WON DEBATE; GREETNG AND LOVE FROM FAMILY; ALL ARE
FINE.
[From] FRANCIS

*[Editor's note: Francis won the coveted Connally Debate Award at Baylor
beating out his usual debate partner Frank Wilson and Harold Knop, the
favorite.*

*"Sophies" were members of the Erisophian Literary Society on Baylor's
campus that Francis was a member of and Frank before him when he was a
Baylor student in the early 1890s. The primary activities of the Erisophian
Literary Society, a men's organization, were debating and speaking
competitively. More about the rich history of Baylor's literary societies will be
included in The Life & Times, the literary societies being first formed when
Baylor was still in Independence, Texas.]*

June 4, 1928 (Monday) [Western Union Telegram]

MRS. F G GUITTARD...PASSED FINAL ORAL EXAMINATION HOORARY THREE HOURS OF PUMMELING LOVE=FRANK.

[Editor's note: Between this telegram and the next communication, there are apparently a number of missing letters. The editor has no explanation for their absence.]

[Editor's note on President Brooks' battles: Despite his earlier position advocating for moving Baylor to Dallas, on June 6, 1928, George W. Truett, a master at raising money for Baptist institutions, in a dramatic softening of his position, in effect pledged his support for Baylor's branches in both Waco and Dallas. While not abandoning his view that Baylor should relocate to Dallas, he tipped his hat to Waco for making an offer to retain Baylor that represented "the greatest challenge that has ever been issued from a city its size..."

Thus, Baylor and its alumni, and Waco and its citizens, both individuals and businesses, had mobilized in common cause to resist the "Dallas" offer. On July 4, 1928, the Baylor Lariat reported that President Brooks had formally opened the Baptist-Baylor drive for two million dollars to support Baylor remaining in Waco. From this date forward, the drive to keep Baylor in Waco gathered steam, a speakers' bureau was organized, a fund raising firm was retained, and financial support poured in from many sources including Baylor alumni, Waco business owners, and non-Baptist churches in Waco. Although monies pursuant to the drive continued to be raised through 1932, that Baylor would remain in Waco seems never again to have been in serious doubt.

Thus, what began as a potential threat to Baylor University at Waco, ironically served only to jumpstart significant expansion and growth. On July 20, 1928, a $100,000 gift was announced from J. L. Kokernot which acted to spur gifts from other wealthy businessmen.]

August 15, 1928 9 p.m. (Wednesday)

Dear Sweetie,

I got all the books you wanted, except one, at the Baylor Library and I will try the public library for that one. I looked thru the list of Roosevelt books and there are 36 in all. They are sending the books directly from the library and they promised me they would get them off today...I feel like you are making splendid progress on your thesis. I am real proud of you. All things good or bad always come to an end.

Sonny [Clarence] and I went to a show this evening and we are just about ready to do to bed...

Lots of love, Josie

[Editor's note: Frank's dissertation topic, "Roosevelt and Conservation," addressed Theodore Roosevelt's affinity for the out-of-doors, forests, rivers, wildlife, and natural beauty, and, inter alia, the actions he took as president to establish national forests and other sites.]

August 22, 1928 (Wednesday night)

Dear Sweetheart,

I had my first, last and only conference of the summer with Dr. Robinson yesterday...He commended the amount of work I have done this summer, then approved my plans, and made some valuable suggestions for the future. It, of course, made me feel good after working all summer as I have. I have always believed in praise and commendations in teaching but shall be more careful than ever as I have realized keenly how much it means.

Lovingly, Frank

August 25, 1928 (Saturday night)

Dear Sweetheart,

As I was coming along the street this evening I noticed this advertisement in a window: "Vacation Special, Permanent Wave $7.50." I was reminded of your first one of a year ago.

Well, well, this is my last letter! What a long time since I left Waco in January! What a year full of work! During this entire time I have had only five full days off; yet I am in better health than when I started in. I have been careful about my eating, exercise, and sleep, as well as breaking the day's work into reasonable periods.....

You have been great in caring for the situation at home. I could never have accomplished what I did without you help. Then you have been kind and sweet in writing so often. Words cannot express my love and appreciation for the part you have taken this year.

Lovingly, Frank

[Editor's note on President Brooks' battles: After the year 1928 closed without as many articles and letters reflecting the persistence of the controversy, the Dallas Morning News at the end of January 1929, published an article with the headline, "Anti-Evolution Bill Opposed," relating to efforts in Texas to get such a bill passed into law.

Ninety years later, in 2018, the question of whether biology teachers in Texas public schools should be allowed to teach evolution theory remains a hotly debated issue in some places as the supporters of creationism and Intelligent Design have taken up the fight previously waged by the fundamentalists.

Baylor's Department of Biology, however, publishes on its website the statement: "Evolution, a foundational principle of modern biology, is supported by overwhelming scientific evidence and is accepted by the vast majority of scientists..." Thus, at Baylor teaching evolution is no longer considered merely an interesting theory that students should be aware of, but an accepted principle of modern biology.]

June 10, 1929 (Wednesday, on the way to Stanford)

Dear Sweetheart,

You certainly were ambitious to tackle an entire bushel of peaches at one time. I know you put up some good eats.

Thanks for all the enclosures and the papers. I do not blame Francis for getting the Ford. I know how I felt when I arrived in East Texas when everybody had a horse and I had none. I had some of the identical experiences until I [got] the horse. It is interesting to note that father and son had about the same reactions to similar situations...Everything is going as usual here.

Francis put up a good argument for his own case [to buy an automobile]. If he does as well for somebody else who places his case in his hands, he ought to win out in the majority of suits...

Lovingly, Frank.

[Editor's note: Regarding Frank and his need for transportation, there is a photo of Frank riding on a horse probably in his 30s. There is also a ledger note confirming that he had a horse after taking the position at Baylor in 1902.

In his lifetime, Frank rode in or on trains, horses, wagons, horse-drawn buggies, bicycles, streetcars, automobiles, buses, and likely inter-urbans. There is no record that Frank ever traveled by ship or flew in an airplane. Frank continued to like hiking for health reasons.]

June 14, 1929 (Friday 9 a.m.)

Dear Sweetheart,

Arrived this morning, had breakfast, settled in my room…my trunk…will be here on a later train…I am ready to roll up my sleeves and make a dive into the work ahead. It has been somewhat like two mules pulling one mule across a ditch but I have gotten across. Had plenty of time to think on my way out here…

Lovingly, Frank.

June 15, 1929 (Saturday)

Dear Sweetheart,

This morning I went out to the University again and saw Dr. Robinson...Dr. Robinson was kind enough to give me a ticket to the Baccalaureate Services...I did not care to see the [Commencement Exercises] again as I had witnessed it last year and believe we [Baylor Commencement Exercises] can beat them...I have unpacked my trunk now and am more settled.

With love and kisses, Frank

[Editor's note on President Brooks' battles: Well-executed homecoming parades and commencement exercises served to promote Baylor University and fell within Frank's interests and extracurricular duties at Baylor, homecoming parades for at least two years (1909 and 1915), and commencement exercises for decades. After the 1915 homecoming parade, Brooks thanked Frank warmly for his key role in the organization and execution of the parade.]

June 16, 1929 (Sunday)

[Dearest Frank]

The hens laid a queer egg today. It was a twin and the shell of each egg was soft. One of them broke when I picked them up but they did not pull apart.

[Josie]

June 19, 1929 (Wednesday 8:30 p.m.)

Dear Sweetheart,

I have had two conferences with Dr. Robinson since arriving. I realize more than ever that I have some steep climbing and difficult digging ahead of me. The only thing that affords a little consolation is that perhaps I have gone through ordeals just as bad before and got out in some fashion…

As my old room was vacated today, I am back in the old place. You know how I like to do things in the same old way, and to wear the same old coat, etc.…It has been rather warm for a few days. I am writing this in my shirt sleeves with all windows up, but it has been cool enough for some heat at night.

Lovingly, Frank.

June 20, 1929 (Thursday night)

Dearest Frank,

We are still missing you but the chickens and I are a bit more reconciled because they offered five eggs for their board today...Clarence is all primed to leave for camp Saturday morning...Don't work too hard...Write.

Lots and lots of love, Wifie

June 21, 1929 (Friday)

Dear Wifie,

Francis seems to be getting oriented in his new environment [Victoria, Texas]. I hope the mosquitos will not inoculate him with malaria. From his program he does not take time out for exercise. I doubt the wisdom of that.

How are the peaches and plums, trees, chickens, lawn, the Buick, etc.?...

I am gathering up the threads where I left off. I had lost some of them. One consolation--I have not had to register which means $63.00 to the good...Well my job gets tedious and tiresome toward the end of the day. I often wonder how long my term of punishment will have to last...

With love, Frank.

[Editor's note: Francis, having graduated from Baylor Law School, was now working for Judge Linebaugh's law firm in Victoria.]

June 21, 1929 (Friday)

Dear Sweetheart,

The [name of a renting couple] have not sent their check. I am trying to get up my courage to phone them today.

From our own vine and fig tree I put up 9 pints of plum preserves yesterday…The car is still a joy. Wish you could enjoy it too…

Lots of love, Josie

[Editor's note: The husband of the renting couple had been a faculty member at Baylor, but had somehow lost his position. Four months later in October 1929, the stock market crashed, ushering in the Great Depression.]

June 21, 1929 (Friday evening)

Dear Lover,

I phoned the [renting couple] and he brought the check over this afternoon. It was dated June 10 and he had been carrying it in his pocket because it was worn. I imagine he is a bit bothered without a job.

I went to the cafeteria for lunch and at supper I ate a sandwich and had a class of lemonade and ate a peach from our trees.

Love and good night, Josie

June 23, 1929 (Sunday afternoon)

Dear Sweetheart,

I have been working most of the day as there is nothing else to do, and it seems just and right that I should devote a little time to my Sweetie, especially when she is always so kind and thoughtful and ready to write to me...

I have found some good material, "dope" in the Palo Alto library so I have not been out to the University for several days. I have been working in my room. Have become a sort of a recluse but, of course, venture out for eats and exercise.

Lovingly, Frank

June 24, 1929 (Monday)

Dear Sweetheart,

Enclosed you will find the check I promised. I hope you can put this away in your savings. I hope too that you will not feel it necessary to rent your own room out for another summer. If the prospective roomers do not like the other rooms available in the house, just let them find accommodations elsewhere. I think in the summer especially you should have the most comfortable room in the house.

[Frank]

[Editor's note: Josie's room on the east side of the second floor was the most spacious of all four bedrooms on that floor, Frank's the least spacious. The size of the two rented rooms fell somewhere in between.]

June 26, 1929 (Wednesday night)

Dearest Josie,

I haven't anything to write about but will write you a few lines to let you know that I am well at present writing and hope you find yourself the same. Glad to get the camp news and to know that the Camper [Clarence] is still doing finely.

Lovingly, Frank

June 27, 1929 (Thursday, from Victoria, Texas)

Dear Mama Josie,

I am absolutely lost in this town without something to ride around in [to] go places... I am in a little play at the Baptist Church. I got in on it to get acquainted with the young people. There are two real nice girls in it. I'd sorta like to give them some attention...Yours truly is just too proud to ask for a ride... I suppose.

The boss's [Judge J.T. Linebaugh's] stenographer...told me I ought to run around more with the kids. She said that I was a regular "old grouch." ...Even one of the married women at the boarding house here said I was a "flat tire."...Without a car I am out on everything...I ought to go to some of these dances here but there is no way to get to the dance hall without walking...There aren't even sidewalks in some parts of town...I would get a Ford or a Whippet roadster. What do you think about the matter?...

With love, Francis

[Editor's note: Francis' talent for advocacy was once again on display.]

June 27, 1929 (Thursday)

Dear Sweetheart,

Clarence is home from camp and outside of a boil in his ear, a blistered back, & red bugs, he is all right. The boil is in the same ear that had one some weeks ago. I took him right down to Dr. Witte and he gave him a puncture…The boil in his ear…seems to be going away; however, to be on the safe side I have taken him to [Dr.] Woosley twice. It is so far inside I can't see it, but the doctor with instruments looked at it and treated it with disinfectants.

The hens are producing fruit every day and they all …seem so happy judging from their songs. The Buick is a joy. The last time I went out to camp I got rained on so I had it washed…

I made 9 glasses of plum jelly and 9 pints of plum preserves from our own fruit and we have a peach occasionally to eat. The hens are producing fruit every day and they all ways seem so happy judging from their songs.

Love, Wifie

June 27, 1929 (Thursday)

Dear Sweetie,

I am glad you did not have to pay tuition...Dr. [William Sims] Allen said that it cost him $500.00 to get his thesis published...He received a 50% royalty ...so he got some of his money back... Do you know anything about the expense of yours? If it costs that much we will have to begin saving on many corners...

[Josie]

[Editor's note: Dr. William Sims Allen, Dean of Baylor's College of Arts and Sciences, was a friend of Frank and Josie. After the death of President Brooks in 1931, Baylor's Board of Trustees appointed him acting president.]

June 29, 1929 (Saturday)

Dear Sweetie,

I wish I could sit in your lap and tell you how much I appreciate the generous check. I hope you have not skimped yourself. I will put some of it in savings. My checking account is a bit low. I have always lived within my income.

Don't think of me as being uncomfortable in the middle room. It is cooler than mine in the mornings. When I take a nap I use the fan, then I have my bath and go down stairs. I think I would like it for all the time. It is so big and roomy and then it joins yours…We have not had many real warm days and all the nights are comfortable. In fact I pull up some cover every night…

Sonny seems to be normal again. He has about caught up on sleep for he sleeps late every morning.

Love and kisses, Wifie

June 30, 1929 (Sunday)

Dear Sweetheart,

Yesterday I went up to the city [San Francisco] to hunt for some books that would help me in my work. I walked my "laigs" weary and then did not find what I wanted. Of course I went out Grant Avenue and found some trinkets for you and Clarence...

You are ambitious to slick up the car these warm days. I think I can use that mop for the top myself to some advantage...

Lovingly, Frank

[Editor's note: On this Sunday an installment of The Bungle Family comic strip was published which, assuming Frank read it while eating breakfast, would have been a reminder of forgetting his June 10 wedding anniversary in 1927; he mentions this omission above in his July 13, 1927 letter to Josie.

The Bungle Family, one of several strips published on Sundays which he read, featured the regrettable but humorous antics of George Bungle who frequently got himself into embarrassing domestic predicaments. The predicament in this Sunday's strip was forgetting his wedding anniversary or his wife's birthday—he could not remember which—only to find out later in the day that it was neither.

If Frank was reminded of the 1927 omission by reading The Bungle Family strip, he does not remind Josie.]

July 1, 1929 (Monday)

Dear Sweetheart,

Clarence came in a few days ago and told me he had put a nail in the chicken yard gate. He said "Mama Josie, Don't you think I am taking Papa's place?"

[Josie]

July 1, 1929 (Monday, from Victoria)

Dear Mama Josie,

I bought the Ford. It is a roadster, and it sure is a keen car. It cost just a little over $600. I thought that since I had decided to remain here next year I might as well get a new car, for it is awfully hard to dispose of used cars in the fall. Everyone has just finished his summer traveling, and the new models of the big cars [have] come out, running the prices of used cars down...

The car runs only 35 miles an hour now, but I can average about 30 easily. I did that yesterday, and a little better. It is about 250 miles to Waco [from Victoria], so that will make about nine hours running time. Coming back I can go a little faster, since I will have limbered the car up more. I will be home about supper time Saturday, so fix me a plate in the kitchen and a bed in the barn...

I don't see how in thunder I can get up my part in the play by Friday of this week but I will bone pretty hard and do it. There are two good looking girls in the play, which makes things worthwhile.

Love, Francis

[Editor's note: Francis, likely through a loan or distribution of trust funds with the help of his Welhausen relatives, was able to obtain the money needed to buy a car.

We suspect Francis was joking about a bed in the barn, even though he had camped out under Spartan conditions in Colorado.]

July 2, 1929 (Tuesday)

Dear Clarence,

Your vacation was like that of a great many people who go away for a summer vacation and then come home to rest up and recuperate, but I know you had a good time in spite of boils and red bugs...I hope you will have a good time the Fourth and that you will not have the experience [Andy] Gump had with his [fire] crackers.

As to your question about my finishing my work, I would only be too glad to tell you if I could. Many students spend a year on their theses I find, and some even more time. I have worked on mine so far about three months. I cannot see the end yet. I hope to be able to do so or to have more clearly in mind the end by the close of the summer...

The little Chinese girl at "the Mandarin" asked about you when I came in for my first meal after getting back.

The walnut tree at my window is loaded with nuts. The squirrel has appeared again after a long absence to try the nuts but they are a little too green yet...

Did you learn any new birds while at the camp? Did you learn any new strokes? How far can you swim? How is the lawn? Are you keeping everything in good shape around the place?

Lovingly, Papa

[Editor's note: The reference to "Gump" was to the central character Andy Gump in a popular comic strip entitled "The Gumps" by Sidney Smith which Frank and Clarence both read. Gump got into many difficult and humorous predicaments, nearly always of his own making.

With Francis working in a law office in Victoria for the summer, Clarence at the age of twelve had taken over some of the household chores.]

July 3, 1929 (Wednesday)

Dear Sweetheart,

An explosion occasionally out in the streets indicates that the Fourth is about here with all its patriotic noise. I shall celebrate as I have for several years—at work in my room as the library will be closed.

As to the expense connected with my thesis, the goal is so far off yet that it seems like a joke to talk about expense...You need not begin to economize yet for a while... Most theses are not worthy of publication. They are of little use or value to the writer and of still less value to the general reader. In fact they are a lot of junk. I expect mine to be somewhat of that class.

Probably you have heard of the student in Zoology who took as a subject for his learned doctor's dissertation "A Study of the Organs of Secretion of a South Sea Turtle." He spent months and months on his investigations; and of what good was it to him or anyone else? There is a whole lot of false value attached to the Degree of Doctor of Philosophy. Would I say the same thing if I had one? Yes, I am pretty sure I would because I have gone through most of the gamut...

Your letters are a great help when I have been digging hard all day and feel rather pessimistic as I am afraid you will characterize this letter.

Lovingly, Frank

[Editor's note: Frank's feelings about the publication potential of his thesis, "Roosevelt and Conservation," might have been different today with the environment being much more prominent in the public eye. For more comment on this subject, see the Epilogue infra.]

July 5, 1929 (Friday)

Dear Sweetheart,

I arrived here three weeks ago today but it seems like months. All days are pretty much the same...

I need a reference. I was so sure that I could get Muzzey's *American History* here that I did not bring my copy. But the copies are out in both libraries here...

With love, Frank

[Editor's note: David S. Muzzey's History of the American People (1927), which Frank used in teaching his classes at Baylor, will be referenced in The Life & Times in a creatively imagined recitation-interrogation based on the first-hand accounts of Frank's former students.]

July 7, 1929 (Sunday)

Dear Sweetie,

Had a letter from Francis yesterday…[he] slept on your bed last night. He said it was so soft he could not go to sleep. How is the thesis progressing? Does the end seem any nearer?…Clarence is very proud of his knife. I got him a chain for it and he wore it today when he left…The chain is a long one that he can fasten to his clothes and carry the knife in his pocket.

Lot's of love—Wifie

I could not help but weep a little after the boys left but they did not see me.

[Editor's note: Francis' statement about the softness of Frank's bed could possibly reflect a gentle ribbing by the younger generation of the older.

As to Clarence and his new knife, knives on chains were popular among boys and men in the 1920s. Frank referred several letters earlier to buying some trinkets on Grant Avenue in San Francisco.]

July 9, 1929 (Tuesday afternoon)

Dear Sweetheart,

I am sure the time passes more quickly with me than with you because I have to do so many different things. Today I read the paper, fed the chickens, fixed my breakfast, washed some dishes, cleaned some parts of the house, answered the telephone, talked to the girls [roomers], went to town, got the mail at Baylor, and had dinner with the Bryans and Mrs. Pogue ....It is now 3 o'clock. What else I may do is not known.

One of the little brown hens is sitting--she won't let me catch her. I tried last night and when she flew away, I put the nest on top of the shed. This morning she was up in the box seemingly quite happy...

I am sure the dissertation does seem quite slow but when you get a bit discouraged and disgusted, just remember how much more you have behind you than before you...

Loads of love, Josie

[Editor's note: The Bryans were the couple at First Baptist Church in Waco who originally introduced Frank and Josie.]

July 10, 1929 (Wednesday)

Dear Sweetie,

I am already to go. If it were not so late, I might start today. Had a letter from Francis yesterday giving me some grandfatherly advice. He said "Don't pick anyone up and for gosh sakes don't drive after night..," neither of which I ever do.

Lotso' love, Wifie

July 10, 1929 (Wednesday)

Dear Papa,

Since I have decided to come back here [Victoria, Texas] next year, I bought a new Ford roadster. They are sure keen cars. They handle mighty easy and have fine shock absorbers. They run like the dickens but squeak like thunder at first...

I was in a play they had here at the Baptist Church. We put it on two times, once at Hochheim and once here last night. It is a rotten play, but I got in it so I could meet some of the people. We won't put in on any more.

I have felt the need of exercise pretty badly, so I bought some golf clubs and joined the country club here. It cost just $25 for membership, so I figured it would be worth it to me, both in exercise and the chance to meet people.

Did you see in the paper where Berkeley Bell of Texas U. won the national intercollegiate singles championship? That puts Texas on the map in tennis. He beat me 6-2, 6-2 at Austin but I could have done much better with practice.

Love, Francis

July 12, 1929 (Friday)

Dear Sweetheart,

Mrs. Johnson [C. D. Johnson] is not so eager to go to her new home but she always works with him [C. D. Johnson]. He says the school has a good endowment, more than Baylor has, has only 350 students and pays good salaries and there are no debts. Has some new buildings and furnishes a brick home, furnished for the President. He did not say so, but gossip says he will get $10,000 and an allowance of $50 per month for entertaining.

[Josie]

[Editor's note: Professor C. D. Johnson, Chair of the Baylor Sociology Department, and his wife, who were good friends of Frank and Josie, left Baylor to accept the position of president at a small college in another state.]

July 14, 1929 (Sunday)

Dear Sweetheart,

I hope you did not have any tire trouble on the way [to Shiner]. I am always afraid of that gravel between Luling and Gonzales. I pass a place often here where they make a specialty of working on speedometers and they have a sign: "Speedometers tested free." I wonder whether it would not be a good plan to have ours tested. It would be an assurance when estimating greasing and draining time....

I hope your dinner was a complete success. I would have enjoyed being with the folks. I don't think I shall really enjoy life again until I get this yoke off my hands.

Lovingly, Frank.

[Editor's note: Bad roads and problems with tires were a source of constant worry for travelers in the early years of automobiles.]

July 15, 1929 (Monday)

Dear Sweetheart,

[Regarding my trip] back, Carl [Welhausen] was driving, did not see a dip [in the road] and hit it so hard he threw us up to the top of the car and my head struck the dome light which proved to be harder than my head so I had to have the wound sewed up in Yoakum...I stayed in the hospital Sunday night at Yoakum just for safety sake...Carl surely did feel badly over the accident, said he had been driving for nineteen years and never had hurt anyone before...

Judge Linebaugh is going to leave Francis in full charge of the [law] office [in Victoria] while he is on his vacation and Francis says he feels so complimented that he would rather stay and have charge of the office than take the trip [to join us]....

Clarence and I had cards from the Chinese girl expressing her appreciation of the cards we sent. She says you like a plain steak almost every night...I have had a number of interruptions since I sat down to write, the phone, door, Clarence, the wash woman, so if the letter seems disjointed you will know why.

Lotso' love, Josie.

[Editor's note: Bad roads and no seat belts made a bad combination. The reference to the Chinese girl is to a waiter at the Mandarin restaurant where Frank often had lunch or supper.]

July 15, 1929 (Monday)

Dear Sweetheart,

I like to write to you at night because I can at least write Goodnight whether I get a response or not. I surely would like to pull the shade down and kiss you goodnight.

Love, Wifie.

P.S. The girls [roomers] have just called from upstairs [renters' rooms on the second floor] [and] said "It is time for everyone to be in bed." We all go to bed early.

[Editor's note: There was always a friendly, almost familial relationship between Josie and the roomers, who were always female. Josie left Hershey bars for them in the refrigerator and likely enjoyed them herself on occasion.]

July 17, 1929 (Wednesday)

Dearest Josie,

Your dinner seems to have been quite a success. My dinners these days are rather simple affairs. As usual to ward off monotony I scatter considerably. I eat at three different places each day ordinarily. Then Thursday and Sunday mornings I go to a good waffle place that I have found...

Francis says in his last letter that he may stay right on at Victoria until school opens. What about the Western trip? Could you and Clarence make it alone?

Lovingly, Frank

July 21, 1929 (Sunday)

Dearest Sweetheart,

You are so nice about writing, I feel that I ought to do better, but there is so little variation in my life these days, that I have nothing to write about. Some days I think I am progressing pretty well, then again I get discouraged at the slow rate of progress, and later things clear up again and so it goes.

Once a week I do take time off to go to the movies. It usually gives me a few hours when I get my mind off my work. I don't care much what they have. They are all about alike. I just go when the time comes...

This is a typical California Day, clear and cool. If it were not for my past experiences of blistered feet, I would be tempted to take a hike to the skyline this morning.

Lovingly, Frank

[Editor's note: Frank may have been downplaying his enjoyment of the hours he spent at the movies in Palo Alto, but possibly not, as he occasionally uses the word "movies" for silent films which tended to be similar and afforded him a chance to sleep if he chose to.]

July 24, 1929 (Wednesday)

Dear Sweetheart,

The only thing new in my household is that I got a pencil sharpener. It will rejoice Sonny Boy, I know, for it is a keen one. I got tired having my hands forever smeared up with black lead. I wish I had gotten one long ago…

With much love, Frank

[Editor's note: On July 25, 1929, Dr. Robinson wrote Frank "wondering how the work on the thesis is progressing" and "I hope everything is satisfactory." He and Frank must have been out of touch for a while.]

July 26, 1929 (Friday)

Dear Sweetheart,

Dr. Witte took the stitches out of my wound [on the top of her head] today so I feel almost as good as new. Only I have to grow some hair because they shaved a good sized spot on my head...

Clarence has an infection from his poison oak that I am having to doctor following Dr. Witte's instructions. The treatments are quite severe so we have some dancing around...The worst place is in the bend of his left arm...

The other night when I was at Henrietta's, I slept in her guest room and I dreamed you were with me and you were when I had been there before...

I know you do get tired of the grind but it will be over sometime; I just hope you won't work too hard. Take some time for your friends and take time to make some new friends. There will be other summers to work. You know about all work and no play.

We are carrying on as best we can at home without you.

Love and a hug and kiss, Wifie.

July 27, 1929 (Saturday)

Dear Papa,

I am getting so I like golf. It is not as simple as it looks. It takes a good deal of skill, and gives good exercise…

I am getting to be a pretty fair hand with the typewriter. Too bad I can't help you with your thesis. I hope you finish it up this summer.

With love, Francis

July 28, 1929 (Sunday)

Dear Francis,

I know your Ford fills a great need. I remember when I came to Texas, every young chap had a horse but me, and I felt about like you did in Victoria before I got my mustang. I hope you are learning the fine points about golf so you can initiate me in return for starting you out in tennis. By the way I do not read the sport page often but I happened to catch the notice about Berkeley Bell's success in tennis...

[Regarding the proposed driving trip to Yellowstone] [it] would be too hard on me and Mama Josie....When I come to the end of August, I shall be greatly in need of rest and quiet for a while...Of course Clarence got weepy when we decided on another plan, but we can go some other time and spend a week in the Park where we have plenty of time...

The work I am doing is a grueling sort of process...in spite of all I can do, I am proceeding with heart-breaking slowness.

With love, Papa

[Editor's note: Berkeley Bell was a highly ranked amateur tennis player from Texas in the late 1920s-early 1930s. He and his partner won second place in doubles at the 1929 U.S. National Championship Tournament.]

July 28, 1929 (Sunday afternoon)

Dear Sweetie,

We are just home from the Bryans. We went home with them after church and had dinner and you are having your nap because it is 4:30 with us and 2:30 with you…

I got 5 eggs yesterday and 3 today, I sold one dozen to the Allens last week. He came down for them and said "these are real hen eggs."

Lots and lots and lots of love——Wifie

July 28, 1929 (Sunday night)

Dear Sweetheart,

In regard to the Western trip, since Francis mentioned the probability of his remaining at Victoria until up to the opening of school in his letter to me, I am going to leave the matter entirely with you. Of course, I do not like the idea much of you and Clarence going alone but probably your trip to Victoria has given you come confidence. If you should prefer to meet me in West Texas or not make the trip at all, it will be satisfactory to me.

Lovingly, Frank

July 30, 1929 (Tuesday)

Dearest Frank,

Hurrah! for the new pencil sharpener, we will all use it when you get home.

How far along is the thesis? Have you passed the note taking stage?...

[Josie]

August 1, 1929 (Thursday)

Dear Sweetheart,

Sorry to hear about your accident. Wasn't Carl trying out the "gaits" of the car? You have certainly had your share of doctoring "sores." You will soon be able to qualify as a skin specialist. This is just to let you know that I am still on the job. If I had more to write, it would be written.

Lovingly, Frank.

[Editor's note: Frank was in a humorous mood here, comparing Josie's auto ride with Carl Welhausen at the steering wheel to riding on a horse.]

August 2, 1929 (Friday afternoon)

Dearest Frank,

Uncle Sam must have had on a slow coach...Clarence had [received] the funny papers on Thursday...

I cannot get Clarence well of all of his sores, though they are better but an occasional new one shows up. ..I am using Dr. Witte's medicines for I have three kinds. I fixed a picnic supper and we ate in Cameron Park yesterday...The scabs have peeled off my wound—So every day in every way I am better & better.

Josie

[Editor's note: Émile Coué, a French psychologist who died in 1926, is credited with recommending the auto-suggestion of saying daily, "each day, in every way, I'm getting better and better" as part of a program for self-improvement and self-therapy. Josie was obviously trying to make Frank laugh.]

August 3, 1929 (Saturday afternoon)

Dear Sweetheart,

I felt like shedding a few tears after reading Rosa's good letter and of course wished we could visit them soon.

You ask about the thesis. Well, there is not much to tell, but I will say what I can, only don't say anything to anybody about it for I have nothing absolutely for giving out. Sometime ago my adviser suggested that I should begin writing and continue my writing and research together. I have followed his suggestion. Up to the present I have ground out about 100 pages of manuscript. This takes up about five chapters and the preface, but there are still six or seven chapters to write and some of them longer than those already written, besides I will be obliged to do considerable investigation for some of them. I have turned in three of the chapters for criticism...

[My] adviser said it was interesting. That was quite an admission for a "hard-boiled" professor to make, but he said enough other things to put that all in the shade. The two most discouraging [were] that it would be well to boil down two of the chapters to one, and that perhaps before I get through, it might be necessary to go to Washington [D.C.] and do some digging in the archives. If he insists on that, I am "blowed up" for I do not know when I could get through...This is not very cheerful news but I thought you ought to know the situation.

So you see there is nothing to give out. I have found that I get along better by writing with pencil on lined paper. I write closer even than in a letter and my pages usually make a page of type written matter. That gives some idea of what I have done. It is slavish work. I would be tempted at times to give it all up if it were not for the fact that you are so nice and loving about writing and carrying on at home.

Probably I should not be discouraged for I was talking to a student the other day who said it took him over three months after he began writing; I have been at it about a month. Then too I had that delay of three months' work on another thesis too which sets me back considerable or rather prolongs the time for completion.

This is not very cheerful news but I thought you ought to know the situation.

Lovingly, Frank

[Editor's note: Frank had an older sister, Rosa, who still lived in Ohio with her family. The editor hasn't found the letter Frank was referring to. Further, the editor hasn't discovered much information about Frank's first thesis topic, his experience with that topic, or why he changed advisers and topics, only that his first adviser was Professor Fish.]

August 6, 1929 (Tuesday morning)

Dearest Frank,

Clarence's sores are improving. As he says he has only a few active ones and we hope to kill them eventually. I don't think he would ever have gotten in such a condition if I had had him with me.

I heard a good story the other day. A man was walking along the street and saw a sign [saying] "Woman's Exchange." He dropped in and when the lady came forward, he said, "Is this the Woman's Exchange?" She said, "Yes Sir." He said, "Be you the woman?" She said, "Yes Sir". He said, "Well, I believe I'll just keep Sallie." Would you feel that way about your wifie?

Love, Josie

August 7, 1929 (Wednesday)

Dearest Josie,

Perhaps Uncle Sam is not so much at fault for the irregularity as your sweetie…I had a terrible spell of absentmindedness the other morning—that is, it must have been from results. I noticed that my shaving did not proceed as well as usual and I came to find out I was using toothpaste for shaving soap.

But more serious, the other morning I missed nearly all the manuscript I had prepared on one chapter of my document. I could not find it anywhere. I had put nearly a whole week on it and some real red blood had gone into it. I looked into all possible and impossible places for it and no manuscript. I began to have visions of having to do all that laborious work over again.

Suddenly I remembered that the landlady had been in my room while I was out for a few minutes and had taken the trash basket down. I rushed down the stairs and roused the lady of the house and calmly as the circumstances would permit asked to see the trash that had been carried down. Lo and behold there it was without a wrinkle in it with some discarded correspondence work. I had been keeping it in the rocker near my right so that I would have it convenient for reference.

As to whether I had put it in the waste basket in an absent minded moment or whether the landlady had absentmindedly picked it up with the rest of the trash I did not stop to speculate or theorize but fervently thanked the Lord and ran upstairs with it.....

Lovingly, Frank

August 7, 1929 (Wednesday afternoon)

Dearest Frank,

I feel quite pleased over the progress you are making on the thesis…Don't work too hard and take time for your friends because there will be some other summers…Tell me some of the material you need and let me scout around for it. Write to the libraries, etc. Just tell me what you need and I will make a try—if I fail to find anything, nothing is lost and I might get some valuable "stuff."…

Really I believe special delivery letters reach me quickest of all…Uncle Sam plays some queer tricks with the mail…

Lots of love for you, Josie

[Editor's note: Frank and Josie's letters tended to contain considerable commentary on the vagaries of mail delivery between Waco and Palo Alto, which are generally omitted from this volume.]

August 9, 1929 a.m. (Friday)

Dear Sweetie,

And still we sweat. I have just wiped up the car so I feel pretty sticky but the car looks so nice after the operation that I feel repaid.

I have had to phone the [renting couple] for the rent since you have been away and they have not paid this month. I thought I would wait a little longer and give them a chance. The month you left I waited until about the 20th last month. I did not wait so long [this time]. I have heard they are a little bitter because he lost his place…

Clarence had his funny papers yesterday that he thoroughly enjoyed as he does all of them. He has only about six active "sores" now. He has some heavy scars on his arm. Dr. Witte said his little girl had the same trouble and has some scars on her face from it.

Lotso' love, Wifie

[Editor's note: Frank enjoyed the funny papers on Sundays in Palo Alto, probably with his Sunday morning waffle. Frank mailed the Sunday funnies to Clarence and thus passed on to Clarence the habit of reading the Sunday funnies. We also mentioned in the preface that Frank on one occasion read the Sunday funnies aloud to the editor in the late 1940s.]

August 11, 1929 (Sunday)

Dearest Lover,

I invited [four friends of Josie] over for lunch with Clarence and me making six of us at the table and [since] Minnie could not help me,…I did all the work. I broiled the chicken and I don't think I ever ate better. Had grape sherbet for dessert. You want me to make you some when you come home? Are you marking off the Sundays? Not many more….

Without telling him I said so, I wish you would write Francis cautioning him about fast driving. He is speed crazy and he drives faster all the time than necessary. After he gets to a place he does not know what to do with his time. I find since my accident I am a little nervous about fast driving and especially on bumpy roads—my head hurts sometimes.

Lots o' love, Wifie.

[Editor's note: Among those coming to the Guittard house for lunch were Dixie Lynn Wood and her mother. Dixie Lynn married Francis several years later. Josie had reported on the collision of her head with the dome light in Carl Welhausen's car in a prior letter.]

August 11, 1929 (Sunday)

Dear Francis,

I do not know when I received a letter that I appreciated more than the last one you wrote. If there is any French in my make-up I suppose it is manifested in my volatile spirits. They go up and then down. When I received your letter they happened to be down.

I have worked hard since coming here, dividing my time between writing and working in the library. So far I have ground out about a hundred pages of manuscript...I write closely on lined paper so when it is type-written it makes nearly a page. But I do not know yet whether it is worth anything, and when I have my doubts, then is when I lose heart somewhat.

I sure have need of a typist. The typist charges from 20 to 25 cents per page including one carbon...

I am glad to learn that you are getting the hang of golf...

With love, Papa

August 11, 1929 (Sunday)

Dear Clarence,

You should have put up a better fight when those girls got after you.

How are your pet sores getting on? How are things looking around the place? Tell me all about something. See whether you can write me a story of three or four or five or six pages on something you have been doing or would like to do.

Tell Mama Josie that the plan suggested in her letter suits me all right. Just let me know when "You all" will be at Albuquerque and where and I will try to make connection as near as possible.

With love, Papa

August 12, 1929 after supper (Monday)

Dear Frank,

I hope the absent-minded professor does not have another hunt for his manuscript...

[Josie]

August 13, 1929 (Tuesday a.m.)

Dear Sweetie,

Hope you got a good typist. Too bad your wife cannot do typing for you. Maybe I should take typing…

Francis and [name of a girlfriend] seemed to have a sort of revival of friendship. I thought for a while [name of another girlfriend] was the choice. The last time he was here he took her picture back with him and now he writes me to send her one of his pictures.

See you ere many moons.

Love, Josie

[Editor's note: Although Frank aspired for both of his sons to learn to type, there is little evidence that he ever aspired to develop the skill himself. Like many people, he seemed to think in cursive with pen in hand when it came to putting his thoughts down in writing.

It appears that Francis had at least three serious girlfriends at one time or another, including Dixie Lynn Wood whom he married in 1933. We suspect Frank and Josie were pleased and perhaps amused that Frank had added girlfriends and dating to his activities (mountain climbing, competitive tennis, guiding at the YMCA camp, debating, typing, shorthand, reading the Bible, and playing the piano) when on prior occasions he had declared a complete lack of interest.

Francis' change of attitude seems to have coincided more or less with his working in a law office in Victoria and acquiring an automobile.]

August 14, 1929 (Wednesday afternoon)

Dearest Frank,

I felt quite pleased over the progress you are making on the thesis. I only hope you won't have the trip to Washington, but if you do, we can go on to Ohio for a vacation afterwards. Anyway, don't work too hard and take time for your friends because there will be some other summers and if you stay alone too much, you never give your mind any rest at all.

[Josie]

August 15, 1929 (Thursday)

Dear Sweetie,

Well Clarence and I are alone. B.U. [Baylor University] closed yesterday and our last paying guest [roomer] left this morning. I like it in the daytime [but] admit it is a bit lonely at night…

Both our small [rent] houses on 7th are being vacated. The [renter couple] move out today and the [other renter couple] soon. [Renter] came over with a sob story and wanted me to take some furniture for this month's rent. I did not do it. He has no place [job] and will go to school on borrowed money. Will send his wife and baby to her mother in California…

[Josie]

August 17, 1929 (Saturday)

Dear Mama Josie,

[Name of girl omitted] has been asking me for a likeness of Yours Truly, and repeats her request in a letter received today. Will you please get one of my pictures, the one without Tux, and send it to me? You can send it with the book, and I can mail it to her or else you can send it straight to the old girl [in Denver]. Much obliged...

My Ford is still running though not as rapidly as it used to run. I am growing a little between the ears. I let two cars pass me coming back from Waco...[On my trip to Port Lavaca] it took 1 hour 45 minutes, where it once took me 57 minutes one night. So you needn't fear my driving. My accident was $24 of good insurance...

With love, Francis

[Editor's note: The exchanging of photos in the 1920s was apparently not unusual when a man and woman wanted to announce their connection, perhaps only to each other, short of engagement.]

August 18, 1929 (Sunday morning before church)

Dear Sweetie,

Hip! Hip! Hurrah! 1407 S. Seventh is rented and I have the check. The people will move in Tuesday. The [non-paying renters] move out sometime next week. Have had several nibbles for their place.

Went down to see my doctor yesterday and she found my blood pressure is up. She asked me what had made me nervous. I told her of my accident: although my wound is healed, my head and neck and shoulder are still somewhat sore. She told me to take things easy and to go on and take my trip but to do it leisurely and come back to see her in October...I will get Will League to care for the chickens and water the shrubs and roses.

Sonny wrote you yesterday while I was down at Dr. Earle's. I had a rather long wait, then she kept me in the office for some time.

Lots o' love, Wifie

[Editor's note: Will League was likely someone who did odd jobs in the neighborhood.]

August 21, 1929 (Wednesday afternoon)

Dear Sweetheart,

I am getting things pretty well rounded out for the trip. I have already had the flashlight fitted out and it is in the pocket of the car....

I certainly agree with you on the vacation. I do not want to tear around until everyone's nerves are on edge. I have already written to Francis and told him such driving would spoil the trip for everyone and in a letter I sent you he seems to agree. I will write him again and mention his golf clubs...

The [former renters'] place is not rented...I don't know just what day the [former renters] will leave. They are selling out most of their stuff but have some things to pack up.

I saw our old blue Buick today. I could not resist opening the door & looking at it. It is a nice looking car.

Love, Josie

[Editor's note: Frank and Josie must have sold their blue Buick and replaced it with another car.]

August 21, 1929 (Wednesday night)

Dearest Josie,

This is my last letter to Waco. I hope it reaches you before you leave...You did some quick work getting the house rented too. The other house is in such good condition it ought to rent well too. Perhaps you could put it in someone's care while you are gone.

Tell Clarence that was a real letter.

Since you will leave Bronte the 2nd, I will leave Palo Alto also the 2nd at 6:50 p.m. and be in Albuquerque the 4th at 2:15 p.m. Do not hurry on the road if you are not there, I will hang up at that hotel, or around there, that you named. If you arrive before I do, you can take in the town. I know it pretty well already—too well, then we can leave the next day probably.

Lovingly, Frank

August 25, 1929 (Sunday morning)

Dear Sweetheart,

I had my last conference [with Dr. Robinson]...I feel better since the last conference. At the first [conference] Dr. Robinson said my work was interesting and then proceeded to land on it with both feet. I did not expect it, of course, but fought back as best I could, however. I came away feeling I had not made much of an impression.

At the second meeting he said the work was interesting and well written and proceeded to land on it pretty emphatically again. I was prepared for him and gave him my interpretation and view of some things...He was very nice and I came away feeling I had made some progress. I think they expect you to defend your work; at least I did some logical talking.

In the last conference when I presented two more chapters...there were a few criticisms of diction and construction and one suggestion about arrangement...Then he said again that my paper was interesting and added "I like your work. I approve of your plan." Of course I felt pretty good, so much so that I took Thursday night off and went to the movies or talkies. I prefer the movies. They are more restful.

Of course, this does not mean that my battles are over. They manage to keep you suspended until up close to the end. I have turned in about 120 pages of typewritten material which have been read and returned. When it is all finished it will be close to 300 pages. So I am not half through writing but it is all outlined and I know exactly what to do when I start in again.

Usually when the adviser approves the work, it is encouraging but then a thesis has to run the gauntlet of the graduate committee at the last and a fellow don't know his fate until up to the last moment. So if anyone should make any inquiries about my work, it would be stating the matter conservatively to say that I seem to be making fair progress. That is about all that can be said or should be said probably. It is best to be conservative.

I have worked hard, scribbling and digging because both must go along together. I shall enjoy a good rest but this last week I will put in some good licks…

I met the Clements too recently. Guess where? Don't say it out loud for it was at the movies Sunday night. We sat together and visited some during the performance.

Give my love to the folks.

Lovingly, Frank

P.S. I should add that Saturday Dr. Robinson phoned me to come out to his home Monday 8 to 10 p.m. to meet the visiting teachers in the Department and some of the older graduate students. I have decided to get out a white shirt for the first time this summer and go.

[Editor's note: By "movies," Frank meant silent films.

Frank's dissertation was approved and bound by Stanford in 1930 and exceeded 400 pages.]

August 26, 1929 (Monday)

Dear Francis,

Well I have one more week left as I shall leave here Monday the 2nd of September…and arrive in Albuquerque at 2:15 p.m. Wednesday, so there will be no need to rush.

I received a letter from Mama Josie saying she had called on her doctor and was told that her blood pressure was up and that she should take it easy on her trip. I thought I should tell you this as she might not care to do so. I suppose it is the result of nervousness following the accident which might have been very much worse. I know you will be careful not to do any hard driving.

It seems to be the natural thing for a young fellow to go the limit when he has a good car. But I think there is always more or less risk in speeding. Machinery is not infallible nor are the human senses nor the common sense of the other fellow. It is of course folly to take risks when there is no necessity for it. As for yourself it would be greatly unfortunate to have to go through life maimed in arm or leg or head or still worse have a promising career snuffed out altogether.

From the papers the "speed devil" seems to be getting in its work out here on the coast. Here are a few clippings [enclosed but no longer available] of what the papers carry daily. I hope you will not take this as "grandfatherly advice," but as a word of caution from one who is more interested in you than anyone else.

My last conference with my adviser was very encouraging and I am feeling better.

I am glad you have decided to be with us.

With love, Papa

P.S. Don't forget your golf sticks. We will hunt up a place where we can use them. Then if you want to read something there is Cheyney's "English History." Every well informed person should know English History, especially a lawyer.

August 26, 1929 (Monday afternoon)

Dear Sweetheart,

I received your two letters this morning and the book Saturday. Thanks for the book. I was thinking of getting a detective story to read—anything to get away from what I have been doing. So I am glad to get the story of New Mexico.

I shall leave Palo Alto Monday September 2nd at 6:50 p.m.....and arrive at Albuquerque at 2:15 p.m. Wednesday. So you need not rush…

Lovingly, Frank

[Editor's note: Other than this passing reference to the detective story genre, we do not know much about what kinds of leisure reading Frank did after he left New Bedford in 1886, not counting the newspapers, Baptist quarterlies and other Baptist materials, the Sunday Funnies, and the Literary Digest. Frank read constantly and broadly.]

August 27, 1929 (Tuesday a.m.)

Dear Sweetie,

Have written you we plan to be in Albuquerque the afternoon or evening of September 3 so if you want to, you can get in the same day we [do] and we will meet at the Franciscan Hotel...At first Francis thought he would rather stay at Victoria, but from his last letters he seems anxious for the trip. He wants to get in a cooler climate...

Hope you got a good typist. Too bad your wife cannot do typing for you. Maybe I should take typing.

Francis and [a serious girlfriend] seem to have had a sort of revival of friendship. I thought for a while [another serious girlfriend] was the choice. The last time he was here he took her picture back with him and now he writes me to send her one of his pictures...See you ere many moons.

Love, Josie

August 27, 1929 (Tuesday)

Dear Clarence,

Your last letter was I think the best one you have ever written to me. It certainly gave me a good idea of how to make good use of old tires.

Last Sunday evening we waited for some time here at Palo Alto to see the Zeppelin, thinking it might honor us with some attention since it was the former home of the President. But we watched in vain for it followed the coast down to Los Angeles and missed out…

I hope that last shot did your sores some good as well as those boils. Maybe the Bronte climate will have a healing effect. Hope to see you all in Albuquerque the 4th [of September] at 2:15 p.m.

With love, Papa

[Editor's note: Frank was talking about Clarence's skill in cutting up strips of old automobile tires to use as projectiles in rubber guns made from ply-wood and clothespins.

The Hindenburg [a Zeppelin] disaster did not occur until 1937. Prior to the disaster, the Zeppelin airship had been developed by Germany, in part, for wartime use. In the 1930s, the Hindenburg flew on commercial flights from Germany to North America. The Zeppelin was named for Count Ferdinand von Zeppelin.]

August 27, 1929 (Tuesday night)

Dear Sweetie,

We had another hot day. My yard is very dry since I had it mowed Saturday and I have run the water too. We had some clouds this afternoon. I would like to have a good shower but I do not want it to come Saturday.

Lotso' love, Wifie

[Editor's note: Josie planned to begin her car trip on Saturday to meet Frank in Albuquerque.]

[Editor's note on President Brooks' battles: The remainder of 1929 continued to conclusion without any additional unusual outbreak of the prior hostilities between J. Frank Norris and President Brooks. The stock market crash in late October 1929 seems to have had no obvious effect on the Brooks-Norris conflict or upon Frank Guittard's pursuit of his Ph.D. at Stanford.

However, at the beginning of the next year (1930), Norris effectively reminded President Brooks that he was not yet through with Brooks, Baylor, and certain other prominent Baptists aligned with Brooks and Baylor. Norris announced to Brooks by letter that he would be attacking Brooks for modernist views and "Dawsonism" as well. In a show of dubious magnanimity, Norris offered to let Brooks speak on the air for an entire day and night.

Joseph Martin Dawson, the long-time pastor of First Baptist Church of Waco, Texas was a friend of President Brooks, and a Baylor classmate of Norris. Dawson claimed that Norris had held a grudge against him that lasted several decades.]

June 2, 1930 (Monday)

Dear Sweetheart,

I arrived here this morning...It is agreeable to get back to familiar quarters but as usual I cringe somewhat at getting down to the exacting work. But I shall be in harness again in a few days.

With much love, Frank

June 3, 1930 (Tuesday)

Dearest Josie,

I am getting settled. I think I did not forget anything except my desk lamp, but fortunately there was one in my room so you will not need to send it...I am glad to know we will have some more of that good jelly. I miss it lots here.

Lovingly, Frank

June 7, 1930 (Saturday night)

Dear Sweetheart,

I have gotten back into the old routine again. It was somewhat discouraging at first. I had to go back and catch up the various lines of investigation where I left them. Had to do some rereading and find that I was a little careless in taking my last notes, thinking I would be able to use them before I left....

I think I have had some good luck...Dr. Robinson told me he would be here this summer...you know I was already set back at least three months with my thesis by changing from Fish to Robinson so I did not know what was in store for me when I came here this time. I handed him chapter VII Thursday as I had completed [it] before I left last summer, but he did not have time to read it. I have nearly another chapter of about twenty pages ready for the typist so you see I have been working some...

[Here Frank reports on his visit with his brother Claude and wife Maud, noting that Maud had a Willys-Knight car.]

If the chickens seem to get along all right, let them stay in their house, but if the heat debilitates them, in other words, seems to affect their laying, then try the open air roost...

Tell Clarence I am depending on him to help keep the place up, weeds, fences, etc. ...

With much love, Frank

[Editor's note: The Willys-Knight automobile was produced during the 1920s in Elyria, Ohio, including both a 4-door sedan and a 2-door coupe.]

June 8, 1930 (Sunday)

Dear Francis,

After some difficulties were overcome I have gotten hold of the various threads where I left them. I looked over your corrections the other night and appreciate them very much. Of course, I had caught some of them in looking over the copy I submitted to Dr. Robinson and had not made them in the carbon copy which you read. But there were some I had overlooked. I find sometimes that I miss an error in looking over a page several times. I wish I could submit the dope to you before turning it in. I need you and Mama Josie as proof readers.

[Finding out that Dr. Robinson would be in residence this summer] This means much to me as I lost at least three months' work by having to change subjects, going from Fish [1st adviser] to Robinson [2nd adviser], and other complications might have arisen had I made another change…

As usual the weather is fine and there is only one thing to keep me from having a good time and that is this downright drudgery of digging and writing a thesis.

I suppose this will find you immersed in legal affairs. Hope you will have time to write occasionally telling of your struggles and triumphs.

With love, Papa

June 10, 1930 (Tuesday night)

Dear Sweetheart,

When I came back from breakfast this morning, what did I find where the folks place my mail? The Anniversary telegram from my Sweetheart! That was sweet and dear of you. I have everything to encourage me to make the most strenuous efforts to get on with my task—your love and interest.

It takes something to hearten the victim of this drudgery. At times I am at it from morning till night and part of the night, in fact most of the times. I am making some progress.

I shall send this by air mail in the morning when I go to breakfast to see if they have improved their schedule. Let me know when it reaches you.

With love and kisses, Frank

June 11, 1930 (Wednesday)

Dearest Josie,

I started in a little too persistently at first [in my work] and it got on my nerves. I found that I could not sleep if I worked continuously, even with occasional intermissions, so I have decided to take at least two nights off during the week, Sunday and Wednesday. Tonight I went to the movie, walked a mile or two, read the paper, took a bath...

I met the little Chinese waitress on the street the other day and asked her if she still worked at the restaurant [The Mandarin]. I think I told you of the elaborate wedding in which she played a leading part last August. To my question she replied, "No, I have a "baybee."

So far I have been out to the university only once. I am working mostly with my notes at present...

Lovingly, Frank

June 14, 1930 (Saturday)

Dear Sweetheart,

Tonight I moved...across the hall to my old room...There is a box seat at one side of the room and I have two tables so I have more room to spread out. I need it when I have to arrange my notes. Then I have room to exhibit my family on the extra table and in their presence I feel more at home....

I certainly would not let anyone have your room for the summer; if they are not satisfied with my room, let them go elsewhere. By the way, if you get anyone for my room, I wish you would take my speech which you will find in the table drawer and put it in some safe place like the cedar chest...I should regret very much to have it destroyed as I put some hard work on it and I may be able to use it again by touching it up with some local color.

Thanks for the book and the papers. I see Governor Moody "does not choose to run."

With much love, Frank.

[Editor's note: This letter is one of several that Frank sent Josie imploring her not to rent out her own room for the summer, hers being much larger and more comfortable than Frank's room, but arguably deserving of a higher rent. Josie tended to be careful in money matters and favored more revenue and less expense whenever feasible.

As to the speech in the table drawer, it is uncertain which speech Frank was talking about although he made several.]

June 15, 1930 (Sunday night)

Dear Francis,

I was glad to get your letter. To hear from someone at home always relieves the feeling I have while am out here that of a sort of an exile. It took a lot of [blank space], what Mama Josie doesn't like to hear us say, to rush away and get out here to my task again. I followed my inclinations last year but I find that it is better usually when you have a disagreeable task to finish it up as soon as possible.

Commencement is in progress here and the graduation exercises will be held tomorrow but I am not attending any of the exercises...

I pass by one of these miniature golf courses on my way to meals occasionally and stop to watch the "putting." I like to get hold of a club myself sometimes, but I know if I did, I would take the time I should be "putting" at something else.

It is needless to tell you to keep up your exercise for I know you will get out on the links whenever you have time for it, but you should not fail to keep up those deep breathing exercises for your health and for your voice.

The number of that prescription is Dr. Cary 100,346 at McKinnon's, Austin Ave. & 6th St. I used a few shots each night before going to bed. I believe it works best not to have it run back in the throat. It does not seem to do so well during the day...

With love, Papa

June 23, 1930 (Monday)

Dearest Frank,

So you are in our old room with your dresser that you like. Would you like the old suit you left in the closet sent out and the old shoes so you can feel real good and comfortable?...I gave the car a good rubbing up Sunday. It looked so nice that Cousin K asked me who was helping my car so beautifully. I bought a long handled mop to clean the top for you know my short arms don't reach so far...

The other day I was in town...I had to go to the bank (church money) before it closed. I was hot as pepper and hungry so I breezed into the cooled dining room of the Hilton and ate lunch. I asked the girl who served me if I might take my afternoon nap in there. She just smiled.

[Josie]

[Editor's note: Frank did not have casual clothes, just newer dress clothes (suit and dress shirt) and older dress clothes. He wore older clothes without a tie when he was dressing informally and wanted to feel comfortable. He did have a pair of knickers which he wore when playing golf.

Cousin K was likely Katherine Bryan who, with her husband Tom, brought Josie and Frank together in late 1919, early 1920.

As seen in this letter, Josie was spontaneously funny. Frank, on the other hand, had a calculated dry wit as seen in other letters.]

June 26, 1930 (Thursday)

Dear Francis,

It is a great satisfaction for me to know that you are able to live above some of the influences with which you come in contact. Many men, to their sorrow and undoing, realize the necessity of following such a course too late in life...

I hope you will [consider] making a speech on Sam Houston someday...especially the unusual and striking things ought to be noted. I find that practically all the speeches one hears on Texas history are trite and a rehash of what every school child in Texas knows. When I spoke to the Lions on George Washington a year or so ago, I adopted the plan of getting away from the usual laudatory style of address. I think some of them did not appreciate my shattering their child ideals of George's perfection of character, but I tried to make it clear that if he was human, as most people do think, it did not detract from his greatness. When I talked to the Daughters of the Republic [of Texas] last year,...I observed the same plan of stressing the unusual. In both cases I got a good hearing...

I wish I could be with you all to enjoy the "glorious Fourth." At that time you may be sure I will be hitting the line as usual.

Lovingly, Papa

[Editor's note: The importance of living "above some of the influences" is a lesson Frank had learned from his own experiences (not specified in the letter), affirming here that Francis' course in this respect had been a "great satisfaction" to him.

Frank was a great believer in planning and living one's life according to a plan; the older he got, the more pronounced his belief in the importance of planning became and the harder he was on himself for not planning sufficiently. In many ways Francis' choices reflect the execution of a plan designed by Frank and which plan Frank would have followed himself had he received early on the advice he had given Francis and the resources to put the plan into effect.

"Hitting the line" is a football metaphor, Frank being the player carrying the ball.]

June 29, 1930 (Sunday night)

Dear Sweetheart,

Just to let you know that I am still "at it."...I sometimes stand at my windows and look out at the deep blue sky, at the eucalyptus trees swaying in the breeze, at the birds as they flit from branch to branch, at the butterflies fluttering from flower to flower, and feel somewhat like a prisoner serving out an unjust sentence with a ball and chain (my thesis) to his ankle, condemned to sit at my table, to dig and write, write, write. Of course, I am making some progress.

General Grant said "I am going to fight it out on this line if it takes all summer." I will have to say the same thing...and leave the "if" out...

I hope you have a patriotic Fourth. I shall scratch out a few more pages that day.

Lovingly, Frank

[Editor's note: On May 11, 1864 during the Spotsylvania campaign, Union General Ulysses S. Grant wrote in one of his dispatches, "I propose to fight it out on this line if it takes all summer."]

July 2, 1930 (Wednesday night)

Dearest Josie,

Today I had my first conference on work turned in. It was that chapter you read. I believe I told you that I did not have time to submit [it] last summer. What transpired at the conference may be summed up briefly. Dr. Robinson said, "It's interesting reading, I have only minor criticisms to make." I submitted two more chapters that I have ground out since coming here. On leaving the conference Dr. Robinson invited me to come out to a luncheon of the graduate students and the professors of the Department of History on the evening of July 10th. I think I shall go.

I feel better since the conference. I think if it has been discouraging I would have felt like "taking out" altogether.

Lovingly, Frank

P.S. Since reading the letter you sent, I think more than ever that my view of the "little girl" is about right. She has all the advantage for she seems to have been through it before. She slyly laughed at those telegrams, in spite of those expressed sincere tears and sadness of heart. Doubtless Francis would feel like kicking himself good and hard if he knew what an easy victim he has been. I have gone through the same program, all of us do, but in my case nobody ever found out what I was suffering, and I would have cut my hand off rather than let the girl know it. For him to do so put him in leading strings and he is hooked good and fast.

As to that encounter with the other fellow, you have not said what kind of an encounter. If the other fellow was the aggressor, and was impudent or insulting, or threatening, he needed to be punched good and hard. As for myself, whether I cared for the girl or not, I would have had it out with him.

[Editor's note: What happened to stimulate Frank's detailed and animated response in the P.S. is unclear, but it sounds like Francis had an unhappy encounter with a girlfriend, perhaps a break-up, and that Francis was upset about it.]

July 6, 1930 (Sunday night)

Dearest Josie,

I am sure the preserve closet must be looking prosperous by this time but you know it is always in demand or its contents.

It seems when Texas Baptists get off on the wrong track in politics, they don't seem to know how to get back. They ought to take a few lessons from the people of North Carolina. You have seen I suppose how they dropped a Hoovercrat (Simmons) who had been in the Senate for 30 years and nominated a good straight dry Baptist Democrat.

I am sending you a clipping from the *Chronicle* of last week. I think I did not tell you that there was quite an epidemic of infantile paralysis or spinal meningitis here last year. It was supposed to have been brought from Hawaii. There are a few houses in town here quarantined on account of scarlet fever, so I am certainly glad Clarence is not here.

The Fourth passed as far as I was concerned without any hilarious disturbance, and even for the rest of the folks in this town as far as I was able to observe.

Nothing unusual is transpiring these days anyhow.

Lovingly, Frank

[Enclosure: Clipping entitled "Help to Meet Menace of Spinal Meningitis"]

[Editor's note: A "Hoovercrat" was a Democrat in a southern state who supported Republican Herbert Hoover in the 1928 U.S. presidential election. This phenomenon was a reaction to the Democrats selecting Alfred E. Smith, previously governor of New York, an opponent of Prohibition and a Catholic, at their convention in Houston to run against Hoover. Senator Furnifold Simmons of North Carolina was among a number of senators including Tom Love of Texas, who supported Hoover.

In Texas, ultra-dry Democrats also opposed Smith. Texas would be counted for the Republican candidate [Hoover] for the first time in a presidential election.

Based on Frank's February 29, 1928 letter excerpted above and others, we conclude that he voted for Smith notwithstanding that he was a Catholic and not favored by hard-line "drys."]

July 9, 1930 (Wednesday)

Dear Sweetheart,

That "Linebaugh and Guittard" envelope looks very professional...

Lovingly, Frank

[Editor's note: Though Francis was, at best, a junior partner, having only worked at the Linebaugh firm a relatively short time, Frank must have been deeply satisfied at the addition of "Guittard" to the firm name. Francis was only twenty-two, barely out of law school, and working in a learned profession, one in which he could potentially make a good living.

Undoubtedly, Frank's guidance of Francis with respect to the choice of a legal career was instrumental in Francis' rapid progress at the firm. In contrast, at the same age Frank was still years away from an entry level teaching position in the Baylor Preparatory Department, which he did not obtain until he was thirty-five.]

July 13, 1930 (Sunday night)

Dear Sweetheart,

Sometimes the harder I work the less results that are to be seen, perhaps it is only my impatience at wanting to get through with all of it. One thing I have to be thankful for and that is that I have been in better health than perhaps ever before while I was out here. I think I have been more careful because so much depends on it. I weighed an even 200 when I first came here but I am gradually remedying that. Don't think I am doing any desperate [attempt] at reducing for I eat at least two good meals a day and never fail to have a good appetite. Walking, of course, is my chief exercise and I never fail to get in some each day.

Lovingly, Frank

July 16, 1930 (Wednesday)

Dearest Josie,

Since the Professor of Latin American History Dr. Martin is still in Spain, Dr. Robinson asked me to prepare a list of questions in that subject for an exam for a candidate for a Masters' Degree. Here the exam is written. I prepared a two hour dose for the poor victim.

It is too bad that "sonny boy" has to pay so severely for his good times at Shiner and you too. It seems to me he is getting old enough to conduct himself differently. He must make up his mind that he cannot keep up with boys older than he is and not with most boys of his age. Why? Well this is the situation and it would be well to talk it into him occasionally. I think he is old enough to understand.

I think I have often told you the he was the most vigorous of the three children when he was born, but the ignorance of his ... nurse very near cost his life. He really owes his life to "Auntie Mama" and should never cease to be grateful to her. This explains his lack of average vigor.

Each one of these sick spells sets him back in his physical development. It is doubtful with his early history if he will ever be a strong sturdy man. He certainly will not be if he keeps having these sick spells. He must understand that if he is to amount to something in this world, he must develop a vigorous body and robust health, probably it is not yet too late. Others have done it. Visits [with relatives in Shiner] should be short or none at all if some self-denial is not practiced in going to bed on time etc.

Lovingly, Frank

[Editor's comment: The details are lost as to the "sick spells" Frank was talking about and the statement about the ignorance of Clarence's nurse. However, Clarence, the "sickly" son, though not particularly athletic, played tennis and golf, taught his own sons to play tennis and golf, maintained a vigorous active life, and lived to be eighty-one years old. Ironically, Francis, the

more rugged, outdoorsy, mountain-climbing older brother, was sixty-three years old when he passed away.]

July 20, 1930 (Sunday night)

Dear Sweetheart,

I still divide my meals pretty well between the Mandarin and the Sunset Cafeteria...and walk a mile or two each day. When I make trips to the Library I walk at least one way. The old street car has been abolished to the University and in town also. Fine large buses have replaced them. The leave for the University every ten minutes.

How are the chickens, the purp, Clarence, and the other inhabitants on the place including yourself?

Lovingly, Frank

[Editor's note: Frank's use of "purp" for "pup" is intentional and we suspect, without any proof, that it stems from a childhood mispronunciation by Francis or Clarence.]

July 23, 1930 (Wednesday night)

Dear Sweetheart,

That was a refreshing remark our friendly neighbor made about your martyrdom and my selfishness in monopolizing this fine climate. Tell her, be sure to tell her, that if she had the choice of taking my job, she would prefer even a still hotter place to live in than Waco. In fact some of the things I have had to go through during the years I have been out here would make h--- itself seem a pleasant place to live in. So tell the old gossip that I am not out here for a summer outing. She needs to be set right...

As to taking time out, that will have to wait...I could not enjoy myself if I did stop a day. It would seem like wasting God's good time, or perhaps better my own. I have taken nearly every Wednesday and Sunday night off but not all, for at times I get impatient to finish something. I am making progress slowly.

Lovingly, Frank

P.S. ...I saw Will Rogers in "So This is London." [O]f course, it was good. Be sure to see it when it comes to Waco...Good night,

With love and kisses, Frank

[Editor's note: It is possible that Josie and Frank's buttinsky neighbor made her remark in an ill-conceived attempt at levity. However, the gratuitous remark did not go down well with Frank who was struggling to finish his dissertation, greatly missing home and family, and very determined that 1930 would absolutely be his last summer in Palo Alto.]

August 10, 1930 1 p.m. (Sunday)

Dear Sweetheart,

As to the thesis, yes, it is much more than half finished. When will I get through? Well I cannot say yet but I think I can finish the writing this summer. I may have to stay somewhat later than usual. I strike a snag occasionally that holds me up.

I do not understand why you should feel as you do about my short letters. I am doing only one thing and see very few people sometimes I hardly speak to anyone all day. I leave my room only to go to meals and exercise, as I go out to the university and work from 8 a.m. to 10 p.m. and only take out a few minutes for dinner and supper. The document room is a good place to work, very few students there, often at night I am the only one. I can spread things out on the wide tables and it is as quiet as in an underground dungeon.

I have a light over me on the ceiling, the rest of the large room is in darkness. The ghosts of the departed statesmen and diplomats, hold their conferences in the dark corners while I dig into their reports, speeches, and communications. The ghosts [of the statesmen and diplomats] don't bother me. I bother their documents. I find that these departed statesmen are pretty good fellows. They had good intentions, for the most part, and contributed their share to the progress of the world.

When closing time comes, I take my grip and walk back to my room through the woods. When the old owl hoots, "Who?" "Who?" I answer back "When?" When will I get through? And it makes me step a little faster.

At night I wake up and the same question comes to me and I resort to my old friend the "Literary Digest" to divert my mind. The first thing I think of in the morning is how long will it take to finish and I hurry and shave and dress to see how much I can do for the day. And so my life is going, working to get through and to get back home. So you see there is not much to write about. Just multiply all my words and lines by ten or more and that represents what my intentions and inclinations are.

Lovingly, Frank

[Editor's note: This letter, which in places is somewhat reminiscent of Edgar Allen Poe, inspired the scene in "A Ph.D.'s Reverie" in which Frank sees an apparition of his mother in the Stanford Library. Frank's use of the term "underground dungeon" in the second paragraph, also a Poe-ish touch (see "The Pit and the Pendulum"), reflects how he felt about still needing to review more documents, an exceedingly tedious task, to finish up his thesis after six summers in Palo Alto.]

August 14, 1930 (Thursday)

Dear Francis,

I received the first letter from Mama Josie since Clarence had his appendix trouble. Of course, it was a great relief to know that he is getting over it. The two telegrams I received Sun[day] morning made me feel very uneasy. I did little effective work that day. I suppose it will be necessary to finish the program of circumcision, adenoids, tonsils, and appendix, to eliminate all physical superfluities.

I am glad to know that you are keeping up your exercise and taking some special chest exercises. That reminds me of some things I have been wanting to write, but first, let me urge you to work on your chest with deep breathing exercises and your chest developer. You know what Roosevelt [Theodore] did for himself along that line.

One thing more: You ask about the thesis. Well, I have gone to the top of the mountain and am coming down on the other side. You know, however, that coming down takes careful climbing as well as going up. So my descent is not on a toboggan or on skis. At times it is too much like the progress of a glacier coming through a gorge. I am pretty well down.

Now for what I started to write. When I take my walks—and I take at least one of a mile or more every day--I think of things which I feel I should have talked with you about before this time, but the last few years have been busy years for you as well as for myself. You know, your mother [Mamie] died of tuberculosis brought on as a result of her weakened condition before and after child-birth [Clarence in 1917]. There was some previous history of the case that I will not go into now. I had a talk with Dr. Witte during those heart-breaking days and asked him what chances the children would have for an average life; to my great relief, he replied, "Better than usual, for you and they will have a better regard for their health." I am telling you this so you need never have any worry about the matter.

However, as any average young man should do, it is the reasonable thing to always care for your health. It is unfortunate that many brilliant young men, are careless about the simple laws of health. They live on the ragged edges, and when a crisis comes, they have no reserves to fight off disease and their lives go out like a snuffed candle.

Above all things, get plenty of sleep. I need plenty and your mother required plenty, nothing seemed to upset her more mentally and physically than loss of sleep. Such matters are largely hereditary. Some people require less than others. I need even now the full eight hours, and of course young people need more. When you are to appear before a jury, you will make a better impression if you are full of vim and pep than if you sat up studying your speech or brief. I am sure this statement is even unnecessary.

One thing more, the old saying "an hour of sleep before midnight", etc., has been exploded, but I find after all there is some truth in it, because intensive work at the end of the day when vital forces are low takes away more vital energy for a given time. I think that is reasonable. In my own case I find it so. I do not sleep well when I am nervously exhausted and I think that is true with anyone who does mental work.

I had hoped to touch the "great question," but I suppose there is time yet.

With love, Papa

[Editor's note: Frank's use of a "mountain metaphor" for his dissertation, Frank ever the teacher, was calculated to resonate especially with Francis. Francis was an accomplished climber of Colorado mountains and detailed his summer mountain-climbing experiences in a number of his letters.

The "great question" Frank referred to likely had something to do with Francis' thoughts about women and marriage. Their discussions of those subjects, and Frank's detailed advice on how to court Dixie Lynn Wood [or any other woman], whom Francis married in 1933, mostly occurred after Frank finished his Ph.D. work in 1930 and thus is beyond the scope of this work.

However, since it is revealing of Frank's strategy in courting his two wives, but especially Josie, one excerpt from Frank's April 17, 1932 letter to Francis might be noted here: "If you find the girl that fills the bill, determine to win her even if it takes time and hurts your pride a little sometimes. Perhaps you have had too easy sailing in some respects and you are not inclined to do your part. But if you win the right sort of a girl, you must do most of the courting." (Emphasis supplied by Frank.)]

August 23, 1930 (Saturday morning)

Dear Papa,

I wish I could be with you today to help you celebrate. It must be a great relief to have all that work off your hands. I know that Mama Josie is overjoyed. It took a lot of guts to through with it all, & if anybody deserves to be called a "Doctor of Philosophy," you certainly do...

When will I be able to read the completed manuscript? And when are they going to christen you?

With love, Francis

August 24, 1930 (Sunday night)

Dear Sweetheart,

I was in the city yesterday. Found exact duplicates of your spoon after trying three or four places...I saw my cousins today...[name of cousin] is the finest of all the girls. [name of another cousin] seems to be a little dippy on religions. She had been one of Aimee McPherson's followers but...is about disgusted with her...by the last sensational doings of Aimee and her mother...

Lovingly, Frank.

[Editor's note: Frank was possibly referring to the strange disappearance of Aimee McPherson in the desert and later her showing up again under suspicious circumstances, all suggesting it was a publicity stunt.]

August 27, 1930 (Wednesday)

Dear Sweetheart,

Awfully glad to get your letter today...It shows that you did not understand my telegram. I sent the same message to Francis and he sent me a rousing letter of congratulation. Your letter said merely: "Just received your message." It made me feel awfully bad after working as I have all these years. I did not get over it for hours.

But your letter today shows you did not get the real import of the telegram. So you see that I was glad to know that you did not understand my telegram, for you could not blame me for feeling badly after going through everything I have and sending a message telling that I had finished my thesis, "finished writing," to be told "Just received your message" and nothing more. So my dear it is not yet too late for congratulations. I know the message was somewhat misleading.

All summer my plan has been to write a chapter, give it to the typist, get it back and proof-read and correct it. The average has been two chapters a week of from 15 to 24 pages. Each week these two chapters of type written material would be given to the Adviser and those of the preceding week returned. This program was followed each week until last Friday [when] I finished writing the last chapter. At that point I sent you the telegrams. The great load was off my mind and heart.

I handed the last two chapters to Dr. Robinson yesterday. Tuesday he asked me to let him have all the preceding chapters as he wanted to read over all of it a second time. He has the entire thesis now—twenty-two chapters—over 426 pages. I will get it all back tomorrow. Then it will be necessary to have it re-typed. The revising is the uncertain element. I do not know how long it will take after I get the thesis back. It depends on how much change is advised and what points have to be looked up.

In the meantime I am putting in every minute, so that when I get the document in my hands again, there will only be the revision and retyping necessary. I am preparing a biography of the author—about a page. This is to be handed in with the thesis. Also an abstract of approximately 1500 or 2000 words on the entire thesis.

Then I also have the bibliography to prepare which is a big task, give exact information of author, title, date, place of publication and publisher of every book used for information in the thesis, a list of magazines with like information, list of government documents, etc. I hope to have the biography, table of contents, the abstract, and bibliography completed by tomorrow morning when I have my final conference, and get the thesis back.

My plan now is to revise it, turn it over to the typist, and pull out for home. The typist will proof-read it, and send it to Dr. Robinson; he will submit it to the graduate study committee during the fall quarter. He has kindly offered to superintend the binding of the thesis for me, and will return my copy, while the University keeps two copies, one for the library and one for the Department of History.

That is the whole story. I am putting in every minute, I even worked late Sunday night...This has been written hurriedly, but I hope I have made everything clear. I was even more disappointed than you that I could not finish sooner, but I have done all a human could. I have never worked so hard and so continuously in my life. The only break during the summer was [Saturday] afternoon and Sunday of last week.

With much love, Frank

P.S. I got some trinkets at Sing Fat's for the Bronte children. I hope the wrapper at Fat's did not get them mixed [up]. It was just at closing time and everything was in a rush.

[Editor's note: The Bronte children were nieces and/or nephews of Josie living in Bronte, Texas.]

August 28, 1930 (Thursday)

Dear Sweetheart,

Had my last conference this morning...Dr. Robinson read it all [again] the second time. Can you imagine how good I felt when he said, "It is an excellent piece of work."...Dr. Fish had also read and approved it.

My task now is to make some suggested revisions, and have it re-typed. I hope to have it ready for retyping by the middle of next week and then I shall pull out for Texas. The typist will send me a copy for proof reading, it will be returned, and Dr. Robinson will submit it to the Graduate Study Committee during the Fall Quarter and have it bound for me. Dr. Robinson said he thought the Committee [would not] make much change in it. With the approval of two hard-boiled professors like Robinson and Fish, I am hopeful that the Study Committee will not find much fault with it.

If any change is made in this program of mine, I shall let you know. Will wire you when I leave.

Lovingly, Frank

[Editor's note: Dr. Fish was Frank's first adviser but a change of adviser was made to Dr. Edgar Eugene Robinson for an undisclosed reason.]

September 26, 1930 (Friday night)

Dear Papa,

Mama Josie asks if I don't want her to make me a bag to put sand from some place, say Magnolia Beach, & then reminisce to my children & grandchildren about where & when I got the sand & tell them not to bust the bag & let the precious sand run out. Tell her that I am not contemplating the proposition of children & I'm not sentimental enough to place any value upon sand, but if she would make the bag, I would be very much obliged, since I haven't something to keep me straight. I don't care what it is filled with...

With love, Francis

[Editor's note: Mama Josie, who could be a kidder, must have been making a joke about Frank Guittard's sandbag eccentricity. Walking erectly with a sandbag on his head was part of Frank's home health regimen to maintain good posture for the benefit of his spine.

Both Francis and Clarence were encouraged to imitate Frank walking with a sandbag, but the practice did not catch on with them and was a source of amusement as much as anything else. Frank, for whatever reason, perhaps the desire to maintain as much credibility as possible for his more serious health advice, did not include this tidbit in his letters of health advice to Francis. We have no similar letters of health advice from Frank to Clarence.]

[Editor's note on President Brooks' battles: By January 1931, J. Frank Norris was no longer pushing his anti-evolution campaign with the same fervor. More on this subject is contained in the "Epilogue" hereinafter.]

[Editor's note on the death of President Brooks, Frank Guittard's receipt of his doctorate, and Brooks' ongoing vision for Baylor: Seven months after the last letter included above, in May 1931, after a brave and prolonged struggle, President Brooks succumbed to his terminal illness. Stanford had conferred a doctorate on Frank Guittard shortly before President Brooks died; Frank formally received his sheepskin at Stanford in June 1931. Frank would

thereafter teach history at Baylor until 1950. Final editor's notes on President Brooks, Brooks' battles on behalf of Baylor, and the continuing vitality of his vision for Baylor are contained in the "Epilogue."]

PHOTOGRAPHS: BAYLOR UNIVERSITY AND LELAND STANFORD JUNIOR UNIVERSITIES

The image or images shown on pages 322-328 are courtesy of The Texas Collection, Baylor University, Waco, Texas.

Rufus C. (Columbus) Burleson (c. 1896).

Baylor student body (c. 1896), outside Main Building with President
Rufus C. Burleson center right on back row.

F. L. (Francis Lafayette) Carroll
(c. 1902).

G. W. (George Washington)
Carroll (c. 1902).

Samuel Palmer Brooks
(c. 1903).

O. H. (Oscar Henry) Cooper
(c. 1899).

Samuel Palmer Brooks (c. 1923).

Georgia Burleson Hall (c. 1896), Burleson Quadrangle, Baylor University, Waco, Texas; Main Building in background.

Maggie Houston Hall (c. 1902), on South 5th Street, Waco, Texas.

Main Building (c. 1919), Burleson Quadrangle, Waco, Texas.

Georgia Burleson Hall (c. 1919), Burleson Quadrangle, Waco, Texas.

Edgar Eugene Robinson, Ph.D. (c. 1923), Frank Guittard's thesis adviser (1928-1930). Permission from the Stanford Historical Photograph Collection.

David Starr Jordan, Ph.D. (c. 1923), President Emeritus of Leland Stanford Junior University. Permission from *The Stanford Daily* and The 1926 *Stanford Quad.*

LOOKING NORTH, WITH PALO ALTO IN THE DISTANCE

Aerial view of Leland Stanford Junior University (c. 1923). Permission from *The Stanford Daily* and *The 1924 Stanford Quad.*

DISCUSSION QUESTIONS AND TRIVIA

These study questions are included primarily for the descendants of Francis ("Frank") Gevrier Guittard and Mamie Welhausen Guittard. It is hoped that the questions will pique their interest in Frank and Josie Guittard's stories and perhaps in biography and history as well. The answers are included in the Appendices. The reference below to "Francis" is to Francis Gevrier Guittard, Jr. The reference to "Josie" is to Josie Glenn Guittard. The reference to "Clarence" is to Clarence Guittard.

Questions from the Poem or the Historical Notes

1. How did Frank happen to take the train from Ohio to Texas in 1886?
2. Why did Dr. Francis Joseph Guittard decide not to move to Texas?
3. Why were orphans sometimes placed on trains in the late 19th and early 20th centuries?
4. What happened to Frank's parents before he could return to Ohio?
5. How did the strange incident in Baylor chapel lead to a job offer for Frank?
6. Where is Stanford University?
7. What happened to Mrs. Stanford's Memorial Church in 1906?
8. What opera had Frank traveled to see on his last trip to Dallas?

Questions from the Letters or the Editor's Notes

9. Why did Frank want a horse in East Texas?
10. What tie did Frank take with him to Palo Alto in 1928?
11. How did Frank develop his good handwriting?
12. Who was Judge West [John Camden West]?
13. What musical instrument did Frank and University of Chicago President William Rainey Harper both play?
14. What railroad did Frank frequently travel from Texas to Palo Alto?
15. What did Frank like to eat on Sunday mornings in Palo Alto?
16. Why did Frank not like to sleep in the room next to his landlady's bedroom?
17. Why did Frank not like staying at a dorm at Stanford?
18. How did Frank find his lost thesis chapter?
19. What was the subject of Frank's thesis or dissertation?
20. What languages did Frank have to master for his Ph.D.?

21. What was Frank's nickname for himself while he was at Stanford?
22. Who forgot his or her wedding anniversary, Frank or Josie?
23. What kind of car did Frank and Josie drive?
24. How did Frank and Josie meet initially?
25. What interests did Frank and Josie share?
26. What special reason did Frank have for marrying Josie?
27. What was Josie's telephone number in Houston in 1920?
28. How did Josie hurt her head?
29. Why did Josie not like to ride in a car with Francis?
30. Who gave Josie driving lessons?
31. What did Josie pay for a gallon of gasoline in 1923?
32. What things did Josie make for her preserves closet?
33. How did the chickens in the backyard pay for their room and board?
34. How did Josie help Frank with his thesis?
35. What jobs did Francis have at the YMCA camp in Estes Park?
36. What did Frank want Francis to do during his free time at the YMCA camp?
37. What Texan did Frank want Francis to prepare a speech about?
38. Why did Francis want a car in Victoria?
39. What was Francis' first car?
40. Why did Francis want to be in a play in Victoria?
41. What did Clarence learn to do at camp?
42. What did Clarence bring home from camp?
43. What color was Clarence's kitty?
44. What were the names of Clarence's dogs?
45. What kind of stories did Frank like to tell Clarence?
46. What did Clarence make from old automobile tires?

EPILOGUE

THE GUITTARD FAMILY

BAYLOR FIGURES IN THIS VOLUME

TUBERCULOSIS, SPINAL MENINGITIS, AND SPANISH INFLUENZA

THE STATE OF TENNESSEE VS. JOHN THOMAS SCOPES & ITS AFTERMATH

THE EVOLUTION CONTROVERSY IN TEXAS

THE EVOLUTION CONTROVERSY IN TENNESSEE & ELSEWHERE

ROOSEVELT, CONSERVATION, AND ENVIRONMENTALISM

A FINAL NOTE ON A PH.D.'S REVERIE: THE LETTERS

THE "PROVERB"

Epilogue

THE GUITTARD FAMILY

Francis ("Frank") Gevrier Guittard, before he died on April 28, 1950, had taught at Baylor University for forty-seven years. He started in the Preparatory Department, sometimes called "The Baylor Academy," in 1902 and then, from 1904 on, taught in the College Department. His total teaching career, including all schools, levels, and subjects combined, exceeded sixty years, and accounted, by one estimate, for over 10,000 students. The overwhelming majority of his students were enrolled in his history courses at Baylor.

Josie ("Mama Josie") Glenn Guittard lived until 1957. Josie was able to make her first and only trip to Europe after Frank's death. Frank never made it to Europe, although he made many trips within the United States and at least one trip to Mexico.

Frank and Josie's joint will established a history fellowship (the Guittard History Fellowship) for graduate students at Baylor University. This fellowship currently provides first-year scholarships in each academic year to the top M.A. student and to the top Ph.D. student. In 2016, descendants of Frank Guittard and Mamie Welhausen Guittard established the Guittard-Verlander-Voegtle History Scholarship for undergraduate history majors.

Both Francis Gevrier Guittard, Jr. and Clarence Alwin Guittard graduated from Baylor University with their bachelor's degrees and then earned law degrees from Baylor Law School, on a six-year plan. Both Francis and Clarence became successful attorneys, Francis practicing in south Texas and Clarence in north Texas. Francis distinguished himself in a number of legal fields, including Texas land titles and related trial work, corporate transactions and municipal finance, and estate planning and probate. Clarence initially excelled as a trial and appellate lawyer in cases involving the law of eminent domain, then as judge of the 14th Judicial District Court in Dallas, and finally as chief justice of the Court of Appeals for the Fifth District of Texas at Dallas. In semi-retirement, he received training as a mediator to help resolve, through the voluntary agreement of the parties, significant disputes that otherwise might have required resolution by judge or jury.

Francis had two sons, one of whom became an in-house attorney for large international concerns, the other a public school teacher and counselor who taught Texas history. Both earned their Bachelor of Arts degrees from Baylor. Clarence had two sons and a daughter. Both sons became attorneys and the daughter a law librarian who married an attorney. Only the oldest son, the editor, graduated from Baylor.

None of Frank and Mamie's great-grandchildren have become attorneys, at least as of the publication of this volume, nor have any of their great-great grandchildren, all of the latter having yet to graduate high school. None have followed Frank's path of choosing the teaching profession.

BAYLOR FIGURES IN THIS VOLUME

Samuel Palmer Brooks (1863-1931) was the president of Baylor University with, as of the time of this volume, the longest continuous service in that office. Called "Prexy" by students, his popularity with students, faculty, and alumni has perhaps never been equaled at Baylor. After the resignation of President Oscar Henry Cooper, Baylor increased in size from several hundred students to several thousand students, and added numerous departments during Brooks' administration. Before Brooks, Baylor was a university in name only, but during Brooks' tenure, it became a real university. Baylor added the College of Medicine, the College of Dentistry, the School of Nursing, the School of Law, and the School of Commerce and Business. Additionally, F.L. Carroll Library and Chapel and G.W. Carroll Science Building, both planned by former President Cooper and in the construction stage, were completed and opened under President Brooks. Brooks Hall, Waco Hall, and Memorial Residence Hall for women were all added to the campus between 1921 and 1930.

With an additional bachelor's degree from Yale following his graduation from Baylor, followed by additional work on a master's at Yale, President Brooks encouraged his faculty in apparently a tactful, implied, Hobson's choice kind of way, to obtain graduate degrees, including the doctorate for department chairs. Numerous Baylor faculty members earned higher degrees at other institutions of learning, often from the University of Chicago. Frank Guittard had just received his master's from the University of Chicago when Brooks offered him a position teaching in the Baylor Academy.

Brooks also strongly defended Baylor during the 1920s when it was under attack by fundamentalists, making use of both his formidable writing skills and his public-speaking skills honed during his college years at Baylor debating for the

Philomathesian Literary Society. In the days immediately before his death in 1931, he left for future generations what became known as his "Immortal Message," in which he left a poignant call to action for all Baylor graduates to care for their alma mater. The "Immortal Message" has become part of the university's lore and has been reprinted many times to commission graduating seniors.

The "Immortal Message" as excerpted affirms:

> *"This, my message to the Senior Class of 1931, I address also to the seniors of all years, those seniors of the past and those seniors yet to be...*
>
> *I stand on the border of mortal life but I face eternal life. I look backward to the years of the past to see all pettiness, all triviality shrink into nothing and disappear. Adverse criticism has no meaning now. Only the worthwhile things, the constructive things, the things that have built for the good of mankind and the glory of God count now...*
>
> *Because of what Baylor has meant to you in the past, because of what she will mean to you in the future, oh, my students, have a care for her. Build upon the foundations here the great school of which I have dreamed, so that she may touch and mold the lives of future generations and help to fit them for life here and hereafter. To you seniors of the past, of the present, of the future I entrust the care of Baylor University. To you I hand the torch. My love be unto you and my blessing be upon you."*

After the death of President Brooks, Frank Guittard for his remaining nineteen years, along with fellow faculty members who shared President Brooks' vision for Baylor, continued to serve the aspirations of their fallen leader. At the time of President Brooks' death, those faculty members included Professors A.J. Armstrong (English), J.D. Bragg (history), J.W. Downer (Latin), Patricia Drake (German), W.T. Gooch (chemistry), Alta Jack (French), E. N. Jones (botany), Andrés Sendón (Spanish), and Henry Trantham (Greek). In fact, President Brooks' dream for Baylor has continued to guide and inspire many more faculty, as well as alumni, students, and administrators who would come after. President Brooks' dream of building a great school has continued to result in progress at Baylor and lives on to the present day, eighty-seven years after his death, with over a century of progress resulting from his leadership and vision as memorialized in his "Immortal Message."

Responding to President Brooks' call, Frank and Josie Guittard on Frank's birthday in 1947, though neither had graduated from Baylor, left the bulk of their estate to Baylor University to create a fellowship for graduate history students. In 2009 the existence of the fellowship facilitated the creation of a Ph.D. program in history. Today the fellowship supports both Ph.D. and M.A. students. Additionally, a scholarship for undergraduate students pursuing history majors has been established by the descendants of Frank and Mamie Guittard.

Pat M. Neff was a close associate, friend, and fellow Philomathesian of President Brooks during their undergraduate days at Baylor. After graduating from Baylor Law School, he became McLennan County's district attorney and eventually governor of Texas (1921-1925). In June 1932, he was asked to succeed Brooks as Baylor's president, a position in which he served until 1947. Neff's accomplishments included further expansion of the Baylor campus and prudent financial management during the years of the Great Depression. Neff was also friends with Frank Guittard and roomed with him for two years in the mid-1890s when they both taught at Southwestern Academy in Magnolia, Arkansas. During that period, Neff and Guittard purchased a set of *Encyclopedia Britannica* together. Later, Guittard traded Neff the pocket watch he won selling books during the summer of 1894 for Neff's half interest in the encyclopedia.

TUBERCULOSIS, SPINAL MENINGITIS, AND SPANISH INFLUENZA

Tuberculosis has plagued the human race since ancient times. It remains the most deadly of all diseases in human history and is spread through the air by an infected person coughing, sneezing, or spitting particles onto another person. Today, infants may be vaccinated against it, although vaccination is rare in the United States. Treatment consists of multiple antibiotics. Vaccinations and treatments for tuberculosis had either not been discovered or had not been made available in the United States until decades after the deaths of Charles Welhausen Guittard in 1916 and Mamie Welhausen Guittard in 1917.

Charles Welhausen Guittard reportedly died from either a complication of infantile paralysis (poliomyelitis) or from spinal meningitis. If he died from spinal meningitis, the disease could have resulted from either polio or tubercular meningitis arising from exposure to tuberculosis, more likely in the editor's opinion. Either way, there was no treatment available for decades. Charles died August 9, 1916, and his mother Mamie died nine months later from tuberculosis of the lungs.

The Spanish Influenza pandemic of 1918 is estimated to have infected five hundred million people worldwide, including 675,000 Americans. It accounted for more deaths of American soldiers than deaths from combat during World War I. The pandemic ended in the summer of 1919. Although there is no record that Frank or Josie Guittard caught the flu, it is likely they were highly concerned about the soldiers returning in 1918 to Camp MacArthur outside Waco who could have contracted the disease. The soldiers returning to Waco may have also been a consideration in when to bring Clarence back to Waco. As a student of history, Frank Guittard would likely have been among a handful of people in Waco who knew that Roman soldiers returning home in 165 A.D. had inadvertently brought the plague back with them.

The Communicable Disease Center (CDC) in Atlanta, Georgia was not established until 1942. Originally created as the U.S. government's response to malaria in the fifteen southern states, the CDC focused on killing mosquitoes. Subsequently, the CDC's mission would gradually extend to all communicable diseases. Since the 1940s, the CDC has been the nation's foremost prevention and preparedness agency. In the last 70 years, the CDC has played an important role with respect to a long list of diseases, inside and outside the U.S., including: Zika virus, Ebola virus disease, fungal meningitis, poliomyelitis, H1N1 flu (swine flu), Salmonella, E.coli, mumps, SARS (severe acute respiratory syndrome), anthrax, West Niles virus, fetal alcohol syndrome, AIDS (acquired immune deficiency syndrome), drug-resistant tuberculosis, smallpox, hepatitis B, Legionnaire's disease, tuberculosis, Asian flu, cholera, and malaria.

Because of the medical discoveries of the 20th century and the work of health organizations worldwide, principally the CDC, none of these diseases, including tuberculosis and spinal meningitis, would afflict the children or grandchildren of Frank and Mamie Guittard, with the exception of Charles Welhausen Guittard who died in 1916 before the cure for tuberculosis was found.

THE STATE OF TENNESSEE V. JOHN THOMAS SCOPES AND ITS
AFTERMATH

Although the Scopes Trial was an actual case in Dayton, Tennessee with real parties, a real judge and real lawyers, it was for the most part a publicity stunt with a carnival atmosphere, orchestrated by special interests and broadcast on the radio to a national audience. The drama was fueled by a number of individuals including celebrities, organizations, the city of Dayton, local business groups, and the State of Tennessee, all with their own special agendas. Initially, some of the citizens of Dayton, along with local lawyers, believed that a trial of one of its public school teachers for teaching evolutionary theory in violation of the brand new Butler Act passed in March 1925, would promote the town. John Scopes, a believer in evolution and a substitute teacher, was recruited to be the defendant. Scopes, who never testified and whose teaching expertise was in math and physics rather than biology, was charged on May 25, 1925 with a misdemeanor, namely, teaching evolution theory to a biology class from a chapter in George William Hunter's textbook entitled *Civic Biology: Presented in Problems (1914)*.

The World Christian Fundamentals Association (WCFA), founded by William Bell Riley, persuaded William Jennings Bryan, an attorney and perhaps the best-known fundamentalist of the 20th century, to serve as a special prosecutor. Bryan ultimately lined up flamboyant fundamentalist Baptist pastor and one-time Baylor professor John Roach Straton as a reserve rebuttal witness for the prosecution, though Straton never testified. The American Civil Liberties Union (ACLU) offered to pay for the defense of anyone prosecuted under the Butler Act. Clarence Darrow, a famous criminal attorney and agnostic who had previously shown disdain for fundamentalism, was brought in for the defense. *The Baltimore Sun* sent journalist Henry L. Mencken to cover the proceedings.

Interested parties supporting the prosecution sought to uphold the Butler Act's prohibition against teaching evolution in public schools, to debunk evolutionary theory, to protect the religious faith of school children who might be disturbed by hearing Darwin's theory advocated or even explained, and to promote the mission of the WCFA. The interests aligned with the defense were similarly complex and included denying that scientists were conspiring to destroy the authority of the Bible, challenging the constitutionality of the Butler Act, protecting the academic freedom of public school teachers to teach their students scientific theories, supporting the morality and ethics of teachers trying to educate their students, and gaining publicity for the American Civil Liberties Union.

Clarence Darrow's primary objective was to debunk fundamentalism by making a laughing stock of William Jennings Bryan whenever possible during the trial. Darrow scored against Bryan especially during his legendary cross-examination of Bryan as an expert on the Bible. As to the defense strategy for Scopes, since the prosecution's case that Scopes had taught evolution appeared almost incontrovertible, the defense's best hope was that after hearing the testimony of defense expert witnesses and arguments of counsel, the jury would simply decline to find Scopes guilty in a jury nullification of the Butler Act. Defense counsel also argued that fundamentalist religion, supported by a minority of Christians, should not dictate what is taught in a science class in a public high school. In the event that the jury declined to find Scopes not guilty, then the defense strategy was to win the case on appeal by attacking the Butler Act.

The case began July 10 and concluded July 25 after only eight days of trial, Judge John T. Raulston having generally denied the defendant's offer of a number of expert witnesses on the Bible. After receipt of the case from the judge, the jury quickly brought in a verdict of guilty. Judge Raulston also levied a fine of $100 against Scopes. On appeal the fine was set aside as the judge legally had the authority to set a fine no greater than $50. After the trial, William Jennings Bryan died within the week. Defendant Scopes went on to graduate work at the University of Chicago, became a petroleum engineer, and lived a relatively quiet life for another forty-five years after the Scopes Trial.

Although it is beyond the scope of this volume to summarize all related legislation by any state and the court cases in state and federal courts, a few comments may be made. Although the interest in the evolution controversy was high during the 1920s and there was considerable legislative activity intended to pass anti-evolution statutes in many states, similar laws were passed only in Arkansas, Florida, Mississippi, and Oklahoma.

By the 1930s, the attention given to evolution theory began to die down. In January 1931, J. Frank Norris was busy planning preaching campaigns in both Amarillo and Houston. The theme of these campaigns, however, would not be evolution, modernism, or heresy at Baptist institutions, but would be a standard pre-millennialism message. By this time Norris was already well-known for preaching against evolution and fundamentalist preachers like Norris, William Bell

Riley, and others, were finding that church members were not as interested in anti-evolution sermons as they had been ten years earlier when the topic was fresh.

By the mid-1950s, all of the principal leaders of the fundamentalist anti-evolution movement were gone from the scene—Bryan (d. 1925), Riley (d. 1947), Straton (d. 1929), and J. Frank Norris (d. 1952). Evolution controversy would not flare up again until interest in the importance of high school science became paramount after the Soviet Union in 1957 launched Sputnik, its first earth-orbiting satellite. With the renewed interest in science, evolutionary theory was again emphasized in high schools. The fundamentalists and other conservative Christians rose up again, this time asserting that creationism, and, two decades later, Intelligent Design, should be taught as viable alternatives alongside evolutionary theory. Court cases ensued and the overall import of the cases, the opinion of most experts, and the weight of public opinion seemed to be that creationism and Intelligent Design were not scientific theories. They were, according to the weight of legal and public opinion, simply religious apologetics for the fundamentalist interpretation of Genesis which did not belong in a public school science class, whether evolutionary theory had become evolution fact or was still only a theory.

Significant court cases pertaining to teaching of evolution theory in public schools have included *Epperson v. Arkansas* (1968), *McLean v. Arkansas Board of Education* (1982), *Edwards v. Aquillard* (1987), and *Kitzmiller v. Dover Area School District* (2005). The Supreme Court in *Epperson v. Arkansas* struck down anti-evolution laws as unconstitutional for violating the Establishment Clause of the First Amendment to the Constitution. The United States district court judge in *McLean v. Arkansas Board of Education* struck down Act 590 of the Arkansas state legislature which required that equal treatment had to be given to Creation Science in schools where evolution was taught. The judge ruled that the law violated the principle of the separation of church and state contained in the First Amendment. The Supreme Court in *Edwards v. Aquillard* held that the Louisiana law requiring public schools to give "equal time" to "alternative theories" of origin was also unconstitutional for violating the Establishment Clause. A United States district court in *Kitzmiller v. Dover Area School District* held that a Pennsylvania school board requirement that Intelligent Design be taught was in violation of the Establishment Clause and therefore unconstitutional. *Kitzmiller* is also authority for the proposition that creationism and Intelligent Design are religious rather than scientific theories.

THE EVOLUTION CONTROVERSY IN TEXAS

Today most, if not all, public and private universities in Texas, including Baylor University, not only allow, but in fact require, the teaching of evolution theory in biology courses as a foundational and unifying principle. Nevertheless, below the college level, the controversy of the 1920s over the teaching of evolution still flares up from time to time, especially where public high schools are concerned. The fundamentalist spirit still survives in the creationist science and Intelligent Design schools of thought, although at the current time court cases throughout the United States have generally favored teaching evolution theory. The modern issues which occasionally surface, often with the support of conservative politicians running for office, are whether schools should also teach the biblical story of creation and whether teachers should encourage students to criticize evolution theory. Non-profit organizations created to support the creationist science or Intelligent Design viewpoint still have a presence in Dallas and Seattle.

THE EVOLUTION CONTROVERSY IN TENNESSEE AND ELSEWHERE

The Butler Act in Tennessee, the subject statute in the Scopes trial, was finally repealed in May 1967, almost forty-two years after the verdict in the Scopes case. In 1975, a Tennessee law requiring inclusion of the teaching of creationism and Intelligent Design along with the teaching of evolution was struck down.

There are a number of states in which anti-evolution legislation with various restrictions tends to be advocated and new bills introduced almost every year. The legislation tends to either mandate that creationism or Intelligent Design be taught along with evolution, that disclaimers be inserted in textbooks stating that evolution is only a theory, that students be required to critique evolution theory when it is presented, or some other requirement the effect of which would be to weaken the credibility of the concept of human evolution. The effect of these mandates would appear, in some cases, to discourage a science teacher from teaching evolution since doing so might invite negative attention from students' parents. Because of the bills' multiplicity, no effort will be made here to track or summarize them.

The battle to restrict science teachers' abilities to teach evolution theory does not appear to be nearing an end and will likely continue, in one form or another, as long as fundamentalists of every variety and certain other extreme conservative Christian groups make up a significant number of voters.

ROOSEVELT, CONSERVATION, AND ENVIRONMENTALISM

Although the cause of conservation in the United States had witnessed several signal accomplishments before Theodore Roosevelt became president (Yosemite Valley in 1864 and Yellowstone National Park in 1872 in particular), it took a giant leap forward in the 20th century during the two terms of the Roosevelt presidency. Roosevelt was responsible for the designation of 150 national forests (150 million acres), 51 bird preserves, 4 national game preserves, 5 national parks, and 18 national monuments, along with creation of the U.S. Forestry Service. Roosevelt had been alarmed that lumber and mining companies were radically reducing the amount of forest land belonging to the public and that large numbers of wildlife were being lost.

Conservation movements were one manifestation of environmentalist movements internationally. The conservation efforts of Theodore Roosevelt in the first decade of the 20th century focused on preserving wilderness and areas of natural beauty, forests, soils, rivers, and wildlife, for hunters, fishermen, campers, hikers, tourists, and all members of the public.

Environmentalism, on the other hand, broadly defined, addressed, and addresses currently, many different issues in the United States, including those associated with industrialization, the growth of cities and urban areas, the proliferation of automobiles and the consumption of fossil fuels, coal-fired plants, coal-heated homes and buildings, smog and contaminated air, contaminated waters from sewage treatment plants and industrial dumping, mercury poisoning, oil spills from wells and tankers, the use of nuclear technology and radioactive fallout, DDT and other pesticides, food additives, climate change resulting from depletion of the ozone layer and excessive greenhouse gas emissions (principally carbon dioxide) produced chiefly by burning fossil fuels, and many other threats to human and animal life which have accompanied humanity's rapid technological progress in the last century. The 1960s, 1970s, and 1980s in the United States were particularly successful decades for environmentalists as the National Environmental Policy Act was passed and the Environmental Protection Agency was created along with other initiatives.

Had Frank Guittard been inclined to publish his dissertation upon receiving his doctorate in 1931, the dissertation might have been interesting to a number of people, including modern day conservation and environmentalist researchers who have written about wilderness areas and the decimation of forests and wildlife. In any event, Frank Guittard's dissertation on Roosevelt and conservation was completed at a time when the scholarly and mainstream literature on the subject was relatively limited, likely one of the reasons the subject was approved by his adviser. 1931 might have been a good year for a book on the state of conservation in the United States and what could have been done to carry that work forward in the 1930s and thereafter.

A FINAL NOTE ON A PH.D.'S REVERIE: THE LETTERS

The Second Edition's projected late 2018-early 2019 publication date has both retrospective and prospective significance. First, 2017 was the 150th anniversary of the year of Frank Guittard's birth (January 7, 1867). Second, the year 2020 will be the occasion of a special celebration of the total number of Guittard History Fellows and Guittard Scholars at Baylor University reaching one hundred. The Guittard History Fellowship awarded its first fellowships in 1959, and the first Guittard-Verlander-Voegtle Scholarships were awarded in 2016. 2020 will hopefully be another year in which the Baylor Department of History will present the Guittard Book Award for Historical Scholarship to a deserving applicant.

2020 will also be an appropriate year to recognize the different challenges Frank Guittard and Baylor University under President Samuel Palmer Brooks each faced during the 1920s or shortly before. Frank's challenges included obtaining a college education without financial support from home, caring for a wife with terminal tuberculosis, caring for a son with terminal spinal meningitis, and then establishing a new marriage, all while performing his teaching and later his departmental responsibilities; finally, beginning in 1923, responding to President Brooks' insistence that department chairs obtain their doctorates. President Brooks' challenges, on the other hand, were many and weighty, but included raising additional monies to grow Baylor in Waco into a larger and more competitive university while defending Baylor and a small number of Baylor faculty members against accusations of heresy lodged by grandstanding fundamentalist preachers. Finally, President Brooks, in the final year of his life, despite the cancer that was ravaging his body, despite being told by his doctors to rest, continued to raise money for Baylor and work tirelessly in its behalf. The 1920s were thus a pivotal decade for Frank Guittard, President Brooks, and Baylor.

THE "PROVERB"

To any reader who may have been wondering, the "proverb" at the beginning of this work is not an authentic proverb of ancient origin. It is rather an exercise of poetic license, a faux proverb, one wholly imagined by the author/editor who, after diligent effort, was unable to find a proverb which epitomizes Frank Guittard's unusual story. However, the names and attributed characteristics of Kronos, Metis, and Tyche are in fact closely drawn from Greek mythology and the conflict noted in the proverb is an extrapolation from the diametrically opposed natures of Metis and Tyche. Where Frank Guittard was concerned, the tension between the urge to carefully plan one's life, on the one hand, and the often unavoidable, inevitable decision to go with the winds of chance, on the other, was quite real and a cause for much later reflection.

APPENDICES
AN HISTORICAL TIMELINE
ANSWERS TO DISCUSSION QUESTIONS
AUTHOR-ILLUSTRATOR COLLABORATION
A PREVIEW OF THE LIFE & TIMES OF FRANK GUITTARD

Historical Timeline for the Principal Characters

- 1845 Feb 1: Baylor University is chartered by the Republic of Texas.
- 1846 Jun: Baylor University opens for college students.
- 1846: Francis Joseph Guittard (FJG) immigrates from France as a family land scout.
- 1856 Oct 2: FJG marries Lydia Myers; parents of Francis ("Frank") Gevrier Guittard.
- 1867 Jan 7: Frank Guittard is born in New Bedford, Ohio.
- 1870 Jan 7: The Waco Suspension Bridge is officially opened over the Brazos River.
- 1872 Sep: First train to Waco arrives in east Waco.
- 1880 Oct 11: Mamie Welhausen is born to Charles and Eliza Amsler Welhausen.
- 1885 Nov 11: Leland Stanford Junior University is founded.
- 1886 Sum: Frank realizes FJG will not be able to pay for his college education.
- 1886 Sep: Frank takes a train to Chester, Texas to scout land for his family.
- 1886 Sep: Baylor University merges with Waco University and opens in Waco.
- 1886-1890: Frank teaches twenty-three months in Texas, six schools altogether.
- 1887 Fall: Frank enrolls at Sam Houston Normal School in Huntsville, Texas.
- 1889 Mar 23: Lydia Myers Guittard dies in Ohio.
- 1890 Feb: Frank enrolls at Baylor University in Waco for the spring term.
- 1891 Oct: Stanford opens for first session adjacent to Palo Alto, California.
- 1892 Oct: University of Chicago opens for its first session.
- 1894 May: Frank's funds run out; leaves Baylor to sell books in Hunt County, Texas.

- 1897 Jun: Rufus C. Burleson resigns as Baylor president.
- 1897 Jul: Frank matriculates at the University of Chicago; stays two quarters.
- 1898: Frank becomes principal of Shiner School; meets Mamie Welhausen.
- 1899 Aug: Oscar Henry Cooper is elected Baylor president.
- 1901 Mar: Frank receives a bachelor's degree from the University of Chicago.
- 1901 Apr: Frank enters University of Chicago graduate school; commits to teaching history.
- 1902 Mar: President Cooper resigns following protest over chapel incident.
- 1902 Apr: Samuel Palmer Brooks is elected Baylor president.
- 1902 May: President Brooks offers Frank a job teaching at Baylor Academy.
- 1902 Jun 11: FJG dies in Ohio; Frank helps settle the estate.
- 1902 Aug: Frank visits Mamie in Shiner, Texas.
- 1902 Fall: Frank begins teaching at Baylor Academy.
- 1904: Frank is promoted to Baylor's collegiate department.
- 1906 Jun: Frank buys a house at 1401 South 7th Street in Waco.
- 1906 Dec: Frank and Mamie marry in Shiner on Christmas Eve.
- 1907 Dec: Francis Gevrier Guittard, Jr. is born in Waco.
- 1910: President Brooks appoints Frank chair of the new Department of History.
- 1915 Feb: Charles Welhausen Guittard, second son of Frank and Mamie, is born.
- 1916-1917: Polio pandemic rages; 27,000 cases in the U.S. with 6,000 deaths.
- 1916 Aug: Charles Welhausen Guittard dies of probable tubercular meningitis.
- 1917 Mar: Clarence Alwin Guittard, Frank and Mamie's third son, is born in Waco.

- 1917 Apr: Mamie is admitted to tuberculosis sanatorium in Albuquerque, N.M.
- 1917 May: Mamie dies at age 36, twenty-four days after being admitted.
- 1918-1919: Spanish influenza comes to Waco; infant Clarence cared for in Shiner.
- 1919 Dec: Frank meets Josie Glenn at Christmas time.
- 1920 Jun 10: Frank and Josie marry.
- 1923 Sum: Frank's spends his first summer at Stanford pursuing a Ph.D.
- 1928 Jan-Aug: Frank pursues his Ph.D. at Stanford.
- 1931 Jun 16: Frank receives Ph.D. sheepskin during Stanford Commencement.
- 1931-1950: Frank continues teaching into his 48th year at Baylor.
- 1947 Jan 7: Frank and Josie make joint will creating fund for history fellowships.
- 1950 Apr 28: Frank dies in Dallas at 83 years of age.
- 1958 Dec 25: Josie dies in Waco at 73 years of age.
- 1959-1960: First Guittard Fellows Ronald Lee Hayworth and Oran Lonnie Sinclair pursue master's degrees in history at Baylor University.
- 2017: First Ph.D. in history from Baylor University is awarded to Brendan J. Payne, Guittard History Fellow.

ANSWERS TO DISCUSSION QUESTIONS AND TRIVIA

1. Frank Guittard took the train to Texas because his family was considering moving to a state where reportedly there was more opportunity to make a living and raise a family than in Ohio. Also, his mother wanted a warmer climate.

2. Dr. Francis Joseph Guittard decided to stay in Ohio because of his age, thinking he was too old to establish a medical practice in Texas.

3. The Children's Aid Society placed neglected or orphan children on trains, intending to find families for them in other cities or states.

4. Frank's mother Lydia died before he returned to Ohio.

5. Frank received a job offer after newly-elected Samuel Palmer Brooks was asked to serve as Baylor University's president. Brooks became president following President Oscar Henry Cooper's resignation. President Cooper had impulsively tossed a small dog out of a window during morning chapel, which action drew a student protest. Brooks, Cooper's successor, and Frank had been in Baylor together.

6. Stanford University was and is in California adjacent to Palo Alto.

7. Mrs. Stanford's Memorial Church on Stanford's campus was seriously damaged by an earthquake in 1906 and had to be substantially rebuilt.

8. Frank went to Dallas to Gaetano Donizetti's opera *L'elisir d'amore (The Elixir of Love)*.

9. Frank needed a horse for routine transportation, there being no automobiles, buses, or streetcars available to him.

10. The only tie Frank referred to in any of his letters was his golf ball tie.

11. Frank developed good penmanship in part because of the emphasis on penmanship in W. W. Franklin's Giant Rhetoric Class at Baylor.

12. John Camden West was an attorney, a Confederate veteran of the U.S. Civil War, a former principal of the Waco Classical Institute, and a supporter of Baylor University in Waco. Colonel West owned land in Waco, which was ultimately transferred to Baylor University and became part of the Baylor campus. He wrote *A Texan in Search of a Fight* about his Civil War experiences.

13. Both Frank and University of Chicago President William Rainey Harper played the cornet at the University of Chicago, Frank in a band and President Harper on occasions when he sat in with the university band.

14. Frank took the Pennsylvania Railroad from Ohio to Texas.

15. Frank liked waffles in the mornings, especially Sunday mornings, often at the Snow White Creamery.

16. Frank on one occasion was disturbed by the snoring of his landlady who slept in a room which shared a wall with Frank's room.

17. Frank preferred a room in a private boarding house because he would not have to hear banjos playing, students singing, and other noisy distractions associated with Stanford underclassmen.

18. Frank found his missing thesis chapter by quickly contacting his landlady and then by looking in that day's trash.

19. Frank's dissertation subject was "Roosevelt and Conservation."

20. Frank had to pass examinations in French and German.

21. Frank's metaphor for what he was doing at Stanford was "digging." He occasionally signed off his letters as "The Digger."

22. Frank forgot their June 10, 1920 anniversary in 1927.

23. Frank and Josie had a Buick.

24. Frank and Josie were introduced by mutual friends, the Bryans, at First Baptist Church in Waco.

25. Frank and Josie's mutual interests were raising chickens, travel, musical performances, raising children, the Baptist Church and its doctrines, spending their income prudently, and Baylor University.

26. Frank needed a suitable partner who would be willing to be a mother to Clarence and make it feasible to bring Clarence back to Waco.

27. Josie's telephone number in Houston was Hadley 4666.

28. Josie, a passenger in Carl Welhausen's automobile, hit her head on the dome light as he was driving along bumpy Texas roads.

29. Francis had a tendency, on occasion when driving an automobile, to exceed the speed limit which made Josie extremely uncomfortable when riding with him.

30. Frank gave Josie driving lessons early on.

31. In Josie's July 10, 1923 letter to Frank, Josie said that she had paid 19 cents per gallon for gasoline.

32. Josie put up fruit preserves of various kinds including plum and peach.

33. The hens laid eggs which Josie sold to friends.

34. Josie helped Frank by finding books he needed for his dissertation and by mailing them to him.

35. Francis carried bags as a bell hop, helped in the kitchen as a cook's helper, and performed work on the boiler gang. Additional tasks included sawing, cutting and hauling wood, as well as cleaning out sewer pipes from the laundry, setting up and carrying stoves, and doing electrical wiring.

36. Frank wanted Francis to prepare himself to be useful in a lawyer's office, including acquiring business office skills such as stenography, typing, and shorthand. He also wanted him to start reading law, *Blackstone's Commentaries* in particular.

37. Frank wanted Francis to prepare an address on Sam Houston.

38. Francis wanted a car in Victoria in order to improve his social life.

39. Francis bought a Ford roadster.

40. Francis wanted to be in a play to meet the attractive girls performing in the play.

41. Clarence learned to swim at camp.

42. Clarence contracted a bad case of poison oak.

43. Clarence's kitty was white.

44. The names of Clarence's dogs were Frisky, Sam, and Billy.

45. Animal stories. Stories in which the main characters were animals, usually dogs.

46. "Rubber" guns. Guns that would shoot large rubber bands Clarence made from old automobile tires.

THE AUTHOR-ILLUSTRATOR COLLABORATION

The illustration of *A Ph.D.'s Reverie* came about as a happy afterthought. The author had been working on *The Life & Times of Frank Guittard*, his grandfather, since 1978 with the hope of eventual publication. However, completion of a life & times, still being in 2017 a far distant prospect despite progress having been made by completing the needed research, the author made a decision. He decided to compose a short biographical poem on Frank Guittard's life and his pursuit of a Ph.D. in particular, simply to have something to show for all the time spent over four decades on *The Life & Times*.

Surprisingly, the author produced a rough draft of the poem fairly rapidly. Then, after revising it multiple times, still being somewhat dissatisfied with it, he obtained the assistance of the Baylor History Department and the Baylor English Department faculty to help him improve the draft and carry the ball into the end zone (the final state of the poem). Then, with an improved draft in hand, he again acted impulsively and submitted it to the 2017 House of Poetry event, and, *mirabile dictu*, it was made the HOP's featured poem. Around the same time, others encouraged him to publish the poem online at *The College of Arts & Sciences Blog*, which he did.

Thus buoyed by the unexpected reception of the poem and then by readers' comments on the *A&S Blog,* the author had an afterthought of the type—"What if illustrations could be added to the poem?" Thereafter the author adopted a more considered plan going forward. Quickly deciding that his own skills at illustration were insufficient, he resolved to find an illustrator willing to take on a small project and then, if the illustrations were acceptable, he would somehow publish the illustrated poem. The trick would be to find the right illustrator, and the right illustrator meant, if at all possible, someone connected with the Baylor Art Department since that would complete a trifecta of Baylor departments working on the poem.

Happily from Baylor Art Department faculty came a strong recommendation of Grace Elizabeth Daniel, an outstanding young art student from Leawood, Kansas, and a meeting was set up for the author and Daniel to discuss Daniel taking on her first professional assignment. In the weeks that followed, the author provided Daniel with photographs of Frank Guittard at various ages along with photographs of his family. Daniel then provided a sample sketch which showed convincingly that Daniel would be a good choice. The terms of the assignment were agreed on. Daniel enlisted her roommate and other friends to pose in various positions suggested by scenes in the poem and took photographs. Then Daniel, with a copy of the poem, the Guittard family photos, and her own photographs, created 15 illustrations in the scattered gaps of time she had to work on a non-credit, non-school project.

The feedback process consisted of Daniel submitting a group of sketches to the author for comment and then, upon receipt of comments, revising and emailing the author her revised illustrations addressing any suggestions made by the author. Nearly all of the illustrations were revised and some more than once. Daniel finished her assignment at the end of 2017, and the author sent his publisher the poem with complementary illustrations and historical notes. The published illustrated poem went on sale at Amazon's website in February 2018 both as an e-book and as a print-on-demand book.

A PREVIEW OF
THE LIFE & TIMES OF FRANK GUITTARD

The Genesis and Goal of a Long-term Project;
The Side Trips Along the Way

First, a gentle reminder to the reader that references to "author" and to "editor" in this work are simply to two different hats worn by the same person. That said, the author's interest in researching and writing a life & times of his grandfather, Francis "Frank" Gevrier Guittard, was piqued in 1978. At that time he came across the first group of what the editor is calling "The Palo Alto Letters." Not long after that, he came into possession of a second group of letters along with other family correspondence and documents. In due course, he made at least twenty-five trips to The Texas Collection at Baylor University where Frank Guittard's papers are housed, found a former Guittard Fellow willing to serve as a research assistant and later as co-editor, and interviewed most of the remaining Baylor faculty members who had been contemporaries of Frank Guittard. The Guittard Papers in The Texas Collection proved to be a treasure trove of information for a life & times work, and included class notebooks from college and graduate school, diaries, letters, essays, ledgers, speeches, autobiographies, and many other written materials, as well as photographs of Frank Guittard and his Ohio family.

After a welcome and timely suggestion by the legendary history Professor Ralph Lynn, the author reached out, first by letter and then by ad in *The Baylor Line*, to former students of Frank Guittard who may still have been alive in 1978-1980. Dr. Lynn made a point of making it clear that it was not then too late to find former students of Guittard, but that that door would be closing soon. Dr. Lynn also admonished the author to remember the words often attributed to Oliver Cromwell, "Paint me as I am, warts and all."

Thereafter, spurred forward, yet chastened, by these sobering words, the author was fortunate enough to be able to correspond with, and receive answers from, seventy-five students who took history courses from Guittard at Baylor, the earliest having taken a course from him over one hundred years ago. The former students' letters, regardless of when the students took courses from Guittard, provided a remarkably consistent picture of Guittard as a teacher of history and a wealth of

357

information about his teaching style, as well as specific incidents that happened in class that otherwise would have disappeared into the past

As a life & times work proved to be, at least in the mind of the author, a project of seemingly Herculean proportions, the completion of which seemed to be only slightly closer to realization in 2016 than in 1978, the author wanted something to show currently for all the time invested in it. Accordingly, he composed "A Ph.D.'s Reverie," a mostly biographical, short narrative poem with accompanying historical notes, to which were added fifteen original illustrations ten months later. Thereafter, the editor then decided that the inclusion of selected family correspondence written during the 1920s would make a logical and meaningful second edition. This Second Edition, along with an editor's preface and an epilogue, would be intended to tie all the pieces together and be more satisfying to graduate students engaging in long-term graduate school programs of their own.

With a life & times work still being the original and ultimate goal, contemporaneous with preparation of the Second Edition, *A Ph.D.'s Reverie: The Letters*, the author/editor started a blog on his Facebook timeline page. He hopes the entries regarding these book projects will be of interest to the reader, particularly to history students working ceaselessly on their theses and dissertations in solitary-like confinement in university libraries.

For those readers of either the First or Second Edition of "A Ph.D.'s Reverie" who are interested in Frank Guittard's story and would like to dig more deeply into his life or his times (1867-1950), *The Life & Times of Frank Guittard* is intended to satisfy that interest. In particular, *The Life & Times* will address the classroom teaching style which he employed for nearly six decades, and also what he was like in moments when he was solely around family or in moments of solitary reflection. Readers, amateur historians in particular, may also be interested in finding answers to one or more of the following questions:

- *What were those crossroads moments* for Frank?
- *What were the high points* in Frank's life? The low points?
- *What decisions* did he have to make as he worked out his career as a teacher?
- *What impact* did the twist-of-fate incident in Baylor chapel in 1902 ultimately have on the course of his life?

- *How was he able*, given his reticent and bookish personality, to successfully sell books door-to-door or to hold the attention of his students?
- *Why did he not return* to Baylor to complete his undergraduate degree when he likely had the money to do so?
- *What was it like to share a room with Pat M. Neff,* future Baylor president and governor of Texas, for two years in Magnolia, Arkansas?
- *How were Frank and Josie* able to afford the large house at 1401 South 8th Street in Waco?
- *Did older son* Francis or younger son Clarence more closely resemble Frank in personality, interests, and inherent ability?
- *What impact* did the untimely deaths of his mother Lydia and the tragic deaths of his wife Mamie and son Charles have on him?
- *What was* the Student Self-Government Association Controversy at Baylor and what was Frank's connection with it?
- *What were the other* controversies on the Baylor campus during Frank's tenure and what role did he play in any of them?
- *What is Frank's lasting legacy*, if any, to his students and to Baylor University?

We would like to hear from readers of this Second Edition or the Arts & Sciences blog or who may be following the progress of this work-in-progress on Facebook, including any students working on graduate degrees, regarding their reactions to Frank Guittard's story, especially to what extent it may have resonated with them.

SOURCES

Sources consulted for the long-term and ongoing project of more than forty years, *The Life & Times of Frank Guittard*, of which this work is an offshoot, have been many and varied. They account for six hundred or more treatises, books, articles in periodicals including those published on the internet, yearbooks, and student research papers (undergraduate papers, masters' theses, and dissertations). They include materials reviewed at The Texas Collection at Baylor University and those acquired from online book sellers, including Amazon.com and Ebay.com, as well as various regional bookstores.

Of course, the papers of Francis ("Frank") Gevrier Guittard, in particular, housed at The Texas Collection in thirty-seven boxes, were invaluable in research for *The Life & Times*, and included letters, diaries, autobiographies, photographs, essays, ledgers, speeches, manuscripts, written exams and humorous answers to exams, academic records, and numerous other pieces of documentation. In addition to the Guittard papers, other archived documents in The Texas Collection were consulted, including issues of the *Baylor Lariat* (student newspaper), volumes of *The Round-Up* (student yearbook) for 1896 and 1902-1950, and issues of other Baylor University publications.

The author/editor personally interviewed the family, extended family, and faculty colleagues of Frank Guittard. The author in the late 1970s-early 1980s also corresponded with seventy-five students who studied history under Frank Guittard during their years at Baylor and responded with their recollections of Frank as a teacher. The students were located through an ad in *The Baylor Line* and by a review of copies of *The Round-Up* for the years 1903 through 1950. The oldest student responding to the ad entered Baylor in 1910, graduated with the class of 1914, and wrote in 1979 that he was Professor Guittard's grading assistant in his senior year. Thus, almost Frank's entire career teaching history at Baylor (c.1904-1950) was represented in the students' responses. Before 1904, Frank taught primarily non-history courses that were part of the Baylor Academy's curriculum designed to get students ready for college.

Finally, many document collections housed at The Texas Collection were consulted which contained letters from, or to and from, Samuel Palmer Brooks, Pat M. Neff, Oscar Henry Cooper, Rufus C. Burleson, Francis Gevrier Guittard, and others. However, nearly all of the Guittard family letters excerpted herein, which are the primary feature of this work, were gathered from family members. Copies of other family letters were obtained from The Texas Collection.

The editor will defer a selective itemization and citation of the sources consulted for the trio of projects (*A Ph.D.'s Reverie*-2018, *A Ph.D.'s Reverie: The Letters*-2019, and *The Life & Times of Frank Guittard*-TBD) until the publication of the bibliography and notes in the last named work, occasionally referred to herein for convenience as *The Life & Times*.

Lastly, mention must be made here of the myriad sources at The Texas Collection consulted for the editor's notes to the letters pertaining to the evolution controversy at Baylor in the 1920s. These included: oral memoirs; letters from the Samuel Palmer Brooks papers, including letters from various Baptist pastors, college and seminary presidents, and faculty to Dr. Brooks and letters from Dr. Brooks to Baptist pastors and others; letters from critics of President Brooks and Baylor University (J. Frank Norris, Dale S. Crowley, and others); issues from many periodicals including *The Baptist Standard, Baptist Courier, Searchlight, Baylor Bulletin, Baylor Literary Magazine, Waco Times-Herald, Waco News-Tribune, Fort Worth Star-Telegram, The Sword*, and *The Pilot*; transcripts of addresses to Baptist conferences; resolutions submitted to various Baptist associations; and a master's thesis addressing the evolution controversy at Baylor University. The Texas Collection, Baylor University, Waco, Texas, also provided the photographic images shown on pages 322-328 herein.

BIOGRAPHIES

CHARLES FRANCIS GUITTARD
GRACE ELIZABETH DANIEL
THOMAS A. DESHONG

CHARLES FRANCIS GUITTARD, AUTHOR AND EDITOR

Charles Francis Guittard, born in Austin, Texas, is one of five grandchildren of Ohio native Francis "Frank" Gevrier Guittard and Texas native Mamie Welhausen Guittard. He is a 1964 graduate of Baylor University in Waco, majoring in English and philosophy. Frank Guittard's choice of law school for his sons Francis Jr. and Clarence effectively continued for one more generation: Charles, his brother John and both of Francis Jr.'s sons Stephen and Philip enrolled in law school. After 20 years practicing law as an advocate, Charles founded the Dallas Bar's Business Litigation Section, but then changed his focus, choosing to serve as a an appointed mediator rather than an advocate in civil litigation. Charles' greatest satisfaction from being a member of the legal profession has been teaching negotiation theory and strategy to law students and coaching them in their skills competitions. In addition to the biographical works in this series, he has written articles for legal journals, including "The Mediator Who Used Hats," "Do Zealous Advocates Manage Conflict," "Conflict Management: The End of Litigation Wars," and "A Prince of Darkness Opens his Bag of Deposition Tricks."

Charles continues to work on *The Life & Times of Frank Guittard* which he began in 1978. He lives in Dallas, Texas with his wife Pat and their dog Maggie. The couple has three children and four grandchildren. Their primary interests are their children, their grandchildren, and their alma maters: Baylor and Centenary College of Louisiana in Shreveport. The poem "A Ph.D.'s Reverie" was featured at Baylor's 2017 House of Poetry.

GRACE ELIZABETH DANIEL, ILLUSTRATOR

Grace Elizabeth Daniel is the daughter of James and Carol Daniel, the eighth of thirteen adopted children. With their love and support, she is currently a senior undergraduate at Baylor University pursuing a degree in both French and Painting. Along with being a member of Baylor's National Collegiate Honor Society and the Baylor French Honor Society, she still finds time to paint and create the art that she loves. Her silver gelatin print "Self Portrait" was chosen for the Baylor Student Art Exhibit in 2016, and her oil painting "Self" was displayed in Baylor's 2017 Student Art Exhibit. She also participated in the Baylor Print Show in both those years as well. *A Ph.D.'s Reverie (1ˢᵗ Edition)* is the first book she has illustrated. In the future Ms. Daniel hopes to continue making illustrations.

THOMAS A. DeSHONG, CO-EDITOR

Thomas A. DeShong is a native Pennsylvanian who has found his way to the heart of Texas. He earned his undergraduate degree in history from Messiah College (2010) and his master's degree in history from Baylor University (2012). At Baylor, he studied American religious history with Dr. Thomas Kidd, with his efforts culminating in his thesis, "American Christianity in the Maritime World: Challenges to Faith in the Early National Period." Thomas has a personal connection to this project. He was the 2010-2011 recipient of the Guittard History Fellowship and helped process Francis Gevrier Guittard's personal papers which are housed at The Texas Collection at Baylor. He resides in Waco, Texas with his wife Rachel and their mischievous cat Minerva. Mr. DeShong is currently Processing Archivist at the W. R. Poage Legislative Library, Baylor University, Waco, Texas.